EX·LIBRIS

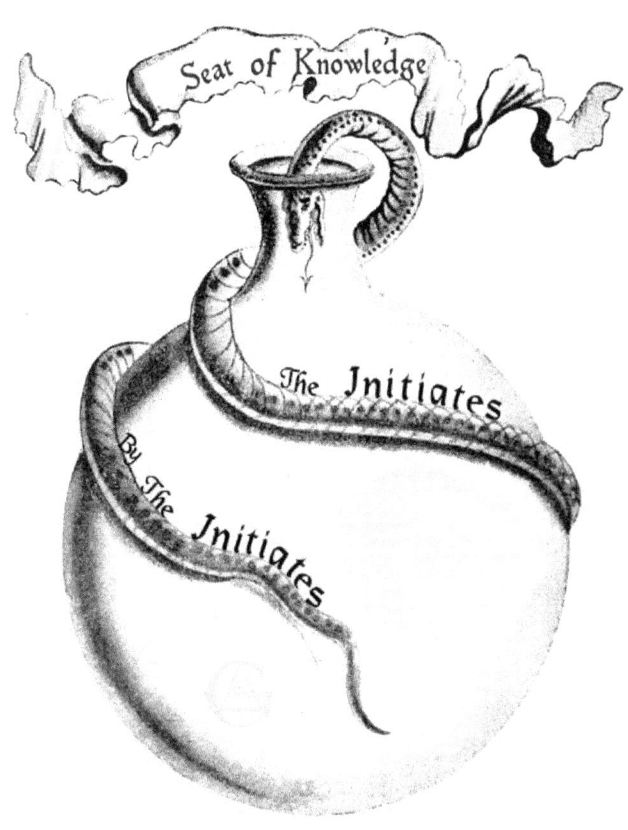
Seat of Knowledge
The Initiates
By The Initiates

The Initiates Speak
Book the Sixth

By: "The Initiates"

Compiled and Edited by
Darrell Jordan 32°

Production Editor
Yuka Jordan

Publisher
Seat of Knowledge

Made in the U.S.A.

Know then thyself, presume not God to scan;
The proper study of mankind is man.
~ Alexander Pope

INTRODUCTION

The growing popularity of True Occultism and Mysticism throughout the whole world has at last induced us to try and issue a series, books that should be an honor to the Universal Father, to True Occultism and Mysticism, and to those who stand for all that is good in humanity. There is also another matter which has induced us to try to see whether such an effort would be appreciated.

This demand we will, therefore, meet, and "The Initiates" will be such a series of which every true student will be proud. We shall not, and will not, cater to that class of sensationalists who would make you believe that by studying a course in hypnotism, which they will sell you for a few dollars, you can be able to make men be your slaves or cause dollars to roll into your hands, for such things are impossible, and not only are they impossible, but it is this class of human ghouls who have brought down shame and disgrace upon a science which holds within itself all the religions ever known.

Not only does Mysticism hold within itself all religious teachings, but it holds the histories of such religions, and it can point the way from the lowest step upon the ladder up to the very highest, which is Imperial Initiation — the finding of the Christ. We shall stand for all that is pure and good in all religious beliefs. We shall try to give to our readers the truth concerning all religious beliefs and will at all times try to get the truth concerning all matters which concern our work. While on the one hand we shall not uphold anything, nor any one whom we know to be a fraud, yet it will not be our desire to tear down any system of thought, but rather to build up a pure and sublime system of philosophy, which shall appeal to the heart of mankind instead of to the mind, as so many do. It is not our desire to destroy, but to build up. Ours shall be an evolution and not a revolution. We believe that we are in a position to give to our readers that which none other can give them, for we are in touch with men and orders in every civilized country in the world, and we are in a position to obtain true facts concerning these matters from any part of the globe, and at short notice.

Regarding the orders of this series, we need only say that the true teachings, so far as they may be given to the profane world, will be given from time to time, and one of our greatest desires is that the old Egyptian religion may be explained in these pages, so that all men, and more especially all Christians, may know that the Egyptian priests did not teach idolatry, but that the people themselves, not understanding the greater mysteries taught, formed idol worship in spite of the teachings of the priests. These are but a few of the things that we shall hope to give to our readers, and all that we shall ask in return is that each and every one truly interested shall do all in his or her power to help and make this series a success. We all know that at the present age of commercialism nothing can be accomplished without the current coin of the realm. It will be our duty to do the work and obtain the material, but we must ask all those who have this great work at heart to do all in their power, so that we may receive the "sinews of war" wherewith to carry on the work, and if all will help in this we can assure each and every one that we will try to give them much more than they pay for.

The Initiates

VICARIOUS REFORMATION

The subject of all worthy legislation is man; the object of that legislation is the improvement of the human state. The insurmountable difficulty to these worthy purposes is the impossibility of the individual actually reforming anyone but himself. Most people are like incorrigible children; and reformatory measures, instead of making them better, simply make them angry. The optimistic reformer should never overlook the fact that there are certain peculiar traits inherent in human nature that have impeded ethical progress since the beginning of time.

The success of any reformation depends upon a single premise: namely, that people want to be better. Of the minority this may be true; of the majority, it is not. Few people have any well-defined desire for self-improvement and of that limited number only a much smaller group has any well formulated plan of procedure. The primary desire of the average man or woman is simply to be comfortable. John Doe wants a fair share of this earth's goods, a little more power than his neighbor, and his name in the Blue Book. He would like to be respected and feared—preferably the latter. He is interested in self-improvement, provided it can be accomplished without effort, sacrifice or discomfort on his own part.

The motion picture industry has suffered from the tragedy of the "educational" film. It is the great box office flop. So past experience has formulated a new procedure to deal with this equation in human nature. If you feel that you must educate the individual, do it without his knowledge; for if he ever suspects that you are trying to improve his intellectual or ethical status he will hate you to the end of his days. The way of the reformer is more difficult even than that of the transgressor. The public mind, restricted by infantile proportions, indulges in infantile reactions. It reasons thus: "Someone is trying to educate me, from which I infer that he thinks I am ignorant. I am insulted—I'll never speak to him again!"

Jane Roe pays fifty cents to see a motion picture. That half dollar she dedicates to entertainment. If she discovers, however, that even five cents of it has been expended to improve her intellectual condition, she will want that nickel back. Culture, like the air, must be free. We will pay to be happy, but not to be wise. The fizzle of radio education parallels that of motion pictures and what we hear broadcasted in the air grows worse every day. There seems to be more or less prevalent the attitude which views it a disgrace to acquire education out of school; in fact, even during school days many only tolerate it because it is compulsory.

Only the minority appreciate learning; the majority must have it thrust upon them, if possible. A man will learn just enough to earn his bread and butter, for a thoroughly buttered slice of bread (whole-wheat) has become the fetish of the average person. Consequently, whenever the problem of actually improving the ethical estate of man comes up, the results are negative, not only through lack of popular support but through actual opposition. John Doe actually dislikes having a better state thrust upon him. He would rather be free to wallow in the mire than to have his Augean stables cleaned up by some method which would curtail or endanger that inviolable aspect of personal liberty "to do as he pleases."

This is an age of progress and, speaking of progress, we are approaching the ultimate reformation. From now on, the trash cans along the curbs are going to be painted gray instead of green. This legislation has been made necessary because people have been posting their letters in these trash cans for years. Educated in our public schools, enjoying our exceptional cultural opportunities, the people who elect our presidents, make our laws and raise our families, the people who are the subject and object of our various reformations cannot yet recognize a trash can when they see one. How can we expect people to enjoy rare intellectual stimulus who consistently post their mail in a box marked "trash"?

Laws are made primarily for people who haven't sense enough to live well without them. These laws protect the person who is either thoughtless of others or who lacks sufficient gumption to take care of himself. The intelligence of the average person is seldom called in question; when it is, as in the problem of the trash can, he falls down hopelessly. As a result, we must have explicit directions for everything that we do. The strip of sandpaper on a box of matches must bear the caption; "Scratch Here," otherwise its purpose would be entirely beyond our comprehension. A door must be labelled "Push" or we might possibly try to get through it with a can opener; and we could not find our way out of a theater if the word "Exit" were not written over the opening in the wall. These little suggestions for our convenience, edification or enlightenment are touching testimonials of what some inventive mind thought of the average intelligence of the human family. And—most lamentable of all—he was right.

The most vicious form of ignorance to be met with is the ignorance which supports selfishness. We have laws governing every human thought and act. These laws are necessary, for they are a Bill of Human Rights by which each person is theoretically protected from the selfishness of every other person. The enforcement of these laws requires an enormous expenditure every year in this country. Hundreds of millions of dollars a year spent to prevent people from injuring, killing and exploiting each other is a startling reflection upon what we please to call our intelligence. But worse still, definite efforts are continually being made to evade these laws and remove all check upon the indulgence of individual ruthlessness.

THE NATURAL RELIGION OF MANKIND

What men ordinarily term religion may be defined as a primitive tradition subjected to constant revision, reformation and restatement. The great world religions of today are products of an almost interminable process of modification. Occasionally the advent of a new religion is announced. If we analyze its articles of faith, however, we will discover that it is only a conscientious objection to some previous cult or creed. Each succeeding religion is built coral-like upon the dead substratum of a previous order. All religious doctrines are interpretations in terms of human limitation of certain ever-existing and unchanging spiritual and ethical realities.

World Saviors are purifiers of tradition, re-shapers and reformers of doctrines. Buddha was a conscientious objector to certain of the tenets of the Brahmans; Jesus was a conscientious objector to certain of the tenets of the Jews; and Mohammed was a conscientious objector to certain of the tenets of the Christians. Conscientious objection is, therefore, the impulse continually arranging into new patterns the fractional parts of religious opinion. We find the reformer of things spiritual in every age and among all peoples. He is endeavoring to reestablish according to his own understanding the natural religion of mankind which has been obscured by false and idolatrous conceptions.

It is, therefore, a mistake to consider religions as essentially different, for the differences apparent in them are wholly superficial and accidental. The philosopher should rather attempt to visualize religion as a life-giving stream whose waters, rising from an unknown source—the splendor of the Eternal Presence—have become polluted from contact with the various civilizations through which they have flowed since the beginning of time. When these waters become the carrier of the poison of perverse opinion and creedal degeneracy, purifying reformations become necessary. These reformations, however, are not directed against the original idea but are simply efforts to return to that idea.

In this century the dilemma has become acute. The departure of theology from its fundamental premises is painfully evident, with the inevitable result that men have turned from the insufficiency of dogma to seek a fuller and more adequate revelation. The prayer of the philosopher today must be, "Let that which is irrelevant be eliminated that the relevancies may be rendered apparent. May the Eternal Truth which is, was and ever shall be, be stated again in terms comprehensible to this civilization."

In every generation there are men who have desired light and who have banded themselves together to investigate the deeper mysteries of God and Nature. These men have been persecuted because their discoveries threatened the integrity of prevailing opinionism. Still they have persisted and many of the symbols of alchemy, Hermeticism and Freemasonry bear witness to their devotion and ability. Max Muller, the German Oriental scholar, stated a fundamental truth when he said that there had never been a false religion unless a child be a false man.

All religions have had one common origin—a desire for greater justice and enlightenment. Most, also, have had a common end. Departing from the simplicity of their origin to become involved in meaningless complexities and dissensions, they have failed from the earth because they no longer served the soul hunger of man. An organization is merely the vehicle of an idea, and when the idea fails or is hopelessly deflected, the organization can no longer justify its right to exist. The Freemason knows that primitive, or natural, religion is consistent with the laws of *Nature* and *God*. That which departs from Nature dies physically and that which departs from God dies spiritually. Only when we abide by the dictates of the Great Father above and the Great Mother beneath can we endure.

Departing from the laws of both Nature and God, temporal religions established an ecclesiasticism which seeks to dictate arbitrarily the destiny of souls. It is this condition that produces the reformer and inclines the mind to the study of such other sciences as can contribute to a new spiritual renaissance. True religion is, in the last analysis, the highest and most perfect form of *natural philosophy*. The deterioration of religion sets in when, turning from the severity of primitive tradition, it attempts to cater to human selfishness. Religions have a tendency to compromise with principle in an effort to increase their own temporal power. This is the beginning of the end, for no religious order has ever survived a compromise. When spiritual truth is sacrificed for the welfare of the organization, then the organization dooms itself to inevitable destruction.

The primitive religion of prehistoric man divided into two main branches, one of which was restated by the Brahmans, reformed by the Chinese, re-emphasized by the Buddhists, purified by the Taoists, moralized by the Confucianists, and transformed into an elemental worship by the Shintoists. Each of these groups endeavored to purge the original revelation of the inconsequentials carried upon the surface of the stream. Each succeeded in some detail but failed in others.

The other branch of the ageless Truth flowed westward to Chaldea and Phoenicia and, abiding for a time in Egypt, raised the Double Empire of the Nile to chief place among the repositories of wisdom. Egypt proved to be a laboratory of chemistry both divine and infernal, and when the stream at last flowed beyond the boundaries of Khem it had lost all semblance of its former appearance. Thousands of years will be necessary to correct the evils originating in the decadent priest crafts of Egypt. To the Egyptian priests we are indebted for nearly all the fallacies of Occidental ecclesiasticism. A battle of truth against error was fought in the dark mysteries of the ancient Egyptians. Truth was supported by the truly enlightened hierophants of the temples, initiates of the great Fire Mystery. Against these was arrayed a pseudo-sacerdotal caste, which probably sprang into existence as the result of the demoralizing influence of barbarians and usurpers brought to the throne of Egypt by war and conquest. These uninitiated foreigners, by virtue of Egyptian law being raised automatically to the chief place in the priesthood but being individually unqualified for such distinction, perverted their religious power and finally brought the Mysteries into disrepute.

Primitive religion thus was lost in a maze of absurdities created by fools, perfected by fools, and finally destroyed by fools. It was in Egypt that religion died and theology was born. Hence, theology may well be termed "a doctrine of usurpers."

THE MUSIC OF THE SPHERES

The Greek philosophers declared all things to have a threefold foundation manifesting through a fourfold constitution. Thus the triangle became the proper symbol of cause and the square the natural emblem of effect. The religious and philosophical systems of Greece were founded upon the teachings of a triad of divinely illumined intellects—Orpheus, Pythagoras, and Plato. Orpheus was the founder of the Greek Mysteries and mythological system. Pythagoras was the master of numbers, music, and astronomy. He overthrew the postulates of the uninitiated Thales, who declared the heavens to be a crystal ball and the stars gilt-headed tacks driven deeply into its surface. Plato was indirectly the disciple of Pythagoras, and most of his writings are based upon fragments of the secret Pythagorean code saved from the burned University of Crotona. When forty-nine years of age, Plato was initiated into the Mysteries of the Pyramid, and was thus "raised" by the same exalted Brotherhood that had sent both Orpheus and Pythagoras into the world. Of all men it was declared that Pythagoras alone could hear "the music of the spheres." He was the first to affirm that music was controlled solely by, and consequently was subordinate to, the laws of mathematics. For this reason Pythagoras believed that it was a mistake to permit harmony to be determined by the ear, declaring that numerical ratios alone constituted its true normative principle.

Pythagorean musicians therefore called themselves Canonics to differentiate their mathematical system of harmonic ratios from the more common Harmonic School of their day, which affirmed the ear to be the final criterion of harmony. So deeply concerned were the Greeks with the laws of musical harmony that they forbade the playing of musical selections which were not dignified and inspiring, declaring that ignoble music endangered the very solidarity of the state. Pythagoras also frequently employed music in healing, and one of his disciples cured afflictions of the nerves and muscles by blowing a trumpet in the patient's ear.

The greatest as well as most sacred symbol of the Pythagoreans was a triangular arrangement of ten dots called the tetrarchy's, which they formed thus:

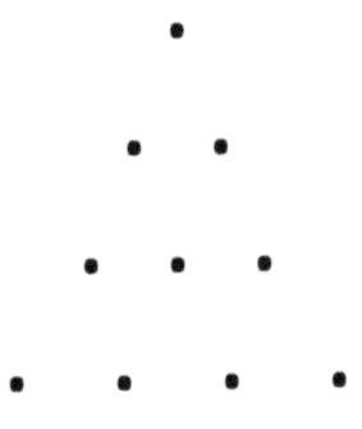

•

• •

• • •

• • • •

Within this triangle of points was contained the sum of philosophy. It was the absolute key to mathematics, astronomy, geometry, music, and cosmogony. The disciples of Pythagoras so revered this emblem that they referred to God as "the One who has given to our souls the mystery of the tetrarchy's." Ten is the sum of the first four numbers (1 plus 2 plus 3 plus 4 equal 10) and represents the creative processes. From the 1 (God) came the 2 (polarity). From the 2 came the 3 (Divine Nature), and from the 3 came the 4 (elementary Nature), thus establishing all creatures and powers.

In his *Life of Pythagoras*, Iamblichus describes the curious incident which first led the seer of Samos to evolve the theory of musical steps or intervals. One day Pythagoras, while meditating upon the intervals of the tetrarchy's, chanced to pass a brazier's shop where workmen were pounding out a piece of iron upon an anvil. By noting the difference in pitch between the sounds of the different hammer blows and their resultant harmony or discord, he gained his first clue to the musical intervals of the diatonic scale. Entering the shop, he found that the difference in pitch was due to the difference in size of the hammers.

After carefully examining the tools and making an accurate estimate of their weights, he returned home and constructed an arm of wood to extend across the room from one wall to the other. At regular intervals along this arm he then attached four cords, all being of the same composition, size, and length. At the lower end of each cord he tied weights of different magnitude to correspond with the different sizes of the hammers.

To the first cord he attached a 12-pound weight, to the second a 9-pound weight, to the third an 8-pound weight, and to the fourth a 6-pound weight. He then discovered that the first and fourth strings when sounded together produced a symphony diapason, or the octave, for doubling the weight produced the same effect as halving the string. The weight of the first string being twice that of the fourth, their ratio was said to be 2:1, or duple. By similar experimentation he ascertained that the first and third strings when sounded together produced the symphony diapente. The weight of the first string being half again as much as the third, their ratio was said to be 3:2, or sesquialter. The second and fourth strings having the same ratio as the first and third, when sounded together also produced another symphony diapente. The first and second strings when sounded together produced a symphony diatessaron. The weight of the first string being a third again as much as the second, their ratio was said to be 4:3, or sesquitertian. The third and fourth strings having the same ratio as the first and second, when sounded together also produced another symphony diatessaron. The second and third strings were said to have the ratio of 9:8, or epogdoan.

Modern efforts to reproduce this experiment have failed. Pythagoras really discovered the harmonic ratios with the aid of a curious instrument having a single string and movable frets, which he termed a Cosmic Monochord.

The first three dots of the tetractys signify the powers resident in the sun, and the remaining seven dots the forces manifesting through the planets—the Elohim of the Hebrews. Of these seven, three are primary and first, and four are secondary and last. The Pythagorean arrangement of the seven ancient planets with their corresponding color and tonal values was as follows:

Saturn Green Fa
Jupiter Blue Sol

Mars Red Do
Sun Orange Re
Venus Indigo La
Mercury Yellow Mi
Moon Violet Si

While differing radically from the modern arrangement, this table has certain points in its favor. The intervals of the first, the third, and the fifth notes of the diatonic scale (Do, Mi, Sol) have as their color correspondences Red, Yellow, and Blue—the primary color tones of the spectrum. Also the seventh note of the diatonic scale, being the most imperfect, corresponds to Violet, the least perfect color of the spectrum, and to the moon whose ray is the least perfect of the sidereal forces.

"The music of the spheres" was the result of three conditions: (1) the magnitude, velocity, and proximity of the celestial body; (2) the keynote of the body itself; (3) the intervals existing between the various heavenly bodies.

Counting inward from the circumference, Pythagoras divided the universe into twelve parts. The first division was called the empyrean, or the sphere of the fixed stars, the dwelling place of the immortals. The second was the sphere of Saturn, the third Jupiter, the fourth Mars, the fifth the sun, the sixth Venus, the seventh Mercury, the eighth the moon, the ninth fire, the tenth air, the eleventh water, and the twelfth earth. Because the octave consists of six whole tones, some authors—such as Robert Fludd, the great English Rosicrucian—have used a double octave to signify these twelve divisions.

The tonal intervals between the planets are as follows: Between the sphere of the earth and that of the moon, one tone; between the moon and Mercury, one-half tone; between Mercury and Venus, one-half tone; between Venus and the sun, one and one-half tones; between the sun and Mars, one tone; between Mars and Jupiter, one-half tone; between Jupiter and Saturn, one-half tone; between Saturn and the sphere of the fixed stars, one-half tone. The sum of these intervals equals six whole tones, or the sum of the tones of the octave.

From the foregoing, the harmonic relationships between the various heavenly bodies may be very easily determined. For example, the harmonic chord between the sun and the earth is a symphony diapente, between the sun and the moon a symphony diatessaron, as is also the harmonic ratio between the sun and the fixed stars. Between the earth and the fixed stars is the most perfect harmonic interval—the octave.

In his History of Philosophy, Stanley shows a single cord stretched between the outer extremity of the starry heavens and the surface of the earth. The planets are placed according to the ancient Greek order, for although Pythagoras recognized the sun as the center of the solar system, he placed the earth in the center of his monochord because his calculations were made from its surface. This reveals what the ancients meant when they spoke of "the seven heavens" through which the soul descends into birth.

The Greek Mysteries included in their doctrines a remarkable concept concerning the relationship of music to form. The elements of architecture, for example, were considered as comparable to musical notes or as having a musical counterpart. The inspired Goethe centuries later said: "Architecture is crystallized music." When a building was erected by the Greeks in which a number of architectural elements were combined, the structure was then likened to a musical chord, which chord was harmonic only when it fully satisfied the mathematical requirements of harmony. Thus a certain chord was said to be the keynote of the edifice. The late Enrico Caruso used to demonstrate this principle of the keynote with a glass tumbler. First striking the tumbler several times to ascertain its tonal pitch, he would then reproduce it with his own voice. After intoning this for a few seconds, the glass would be shattered to bits. In all likelihood, this is the true explanation of the story of the walls of Jericho which fell when the trumpets of Israel were sounded. By applying the same principle (in a manner now unknown), a disciple of Pythagoras once prevented a guest from murdering his host. After striking a few notes upon a lyre, the angry man with drawn sword trembled like a leaf and was unable to move until the musician ceased his playing.

THOUGHT FORCES

Anyone understanding the value of thought forces and suggestion can help the ignorant and the irresponsible to a better condition of life. These forces are understood alike by the just and the unjust in the psychic realms, just as all scientific principles are applied by the true physician to heal, or the grafting doctor to prolong the case and extort fees. The man whose physical health has become dependent upon his physician is to be pitied, but he is a free man compared to that one whose mental health is undermined and obsessed by the grafting hypnotist and fake palmist.

Good does grow out of seeming evil and the victim who awakens even by such terrible means to the power and potency of mind force has advanced toward the solution of his own life problems. But if he can be so hypnotized as to believe that the "professor" is doing the work for him, his case is worse than before.

In the earlier stages of undeveloped mediumship, the medium, not understanding his danger is frequently the victim of the hypnotist in everyday life. Sometimes fully, sometimes only slightly, but if in any degree under hypnotic domination he will do and say things apparently of his own volition that are really inspired by malicious magnetism directed by persons even at a distance. This explains why many people do not realize their earlier promise. Also why some seemingly beautiful and truthful souls exhibit a fatal weakness or falling away from principle. This falling away will be only temporary or until the victim is able to throw off the influence of the hypnotist. This will be through some shock of awakening or through the strong counter-suggestion of someone who sees what the victim is unconscious of. Every human consciousness comes under hypnotic suggestion and domination of some friend, relative or associate at least once in his life. Not till he awakens to the fact and consciously repels the power of hypnotic forces is he free from the dangers of this evil.

All evil emanates through hypnotic suggestion. Every species of crime and all forms of graft are the visible result of this power. The very desire to steal comes from a sort of hypnotic suggestion to acquire by stealth or force what does not rightfully belong to the thief. The grafter is the victim of the hypnotic suggestion of sloth and dishonesty, to acquire that easily which it would otherwise take much labor to earn. The manufacturer of near-silver products costing a few cents and frequently foisted upon an ignorant or unsuspecting victim as "sterling" is a victim of the hypnotic suggestions of greed and dishonesty, and that sly phrase, "Who will know?" In the stores, in the shops, everywhere we find graft, graft, and dishonest valuations. Watered stocks, and inflated banking reports, big promises and small performances, these are all graft and all the result of the hypnotic suggestion of the example around and about each and every field of competitive labor and industry.

Greed for gold seems to be the motive of hypnotic suggestion in every sort of graft. Politicians, police, judges and jurors, men, women and little children, all are caught by the golden gleam and with the eyes fastened on this glittering object the victim is drawn, he knows not how, into strange paths and questionable methods. The fake newspaper story is the result of the golden reward for something unusual, the writer opens his soul and mind to suggestion or inspiration. But, ah, the hypnotic suggestion has already been made that it must be sensational and remarkable. Never mind the truth. It will go.

The instant he lets go of truth, his inspiration is gone, but hypnotic suggestions unnumbered crowd in upon his weary brain and so another useless story, too often suggestive in its turn of all that is evil, or at least un-elevating, goes out into the world. The writer does not want to fake, but after a while he is called so clever, so original; so he begins to find faking both pleasant and profitable. If his soul revolts now and then, the hypnotic suggestion of the world's applause, and the golden return is there to lull his conscience. Do you wonder, then, when statesmen and presidents and writers and ministers of the gospel even descend to graft, prostituting noble intellects and cultured minds, that the ignorant, helpless, wandering children of every dime and race with no training, no knowledge seize upon the grafting methods that appeal to their own limited intelligence and so the game goes on. Lower, lower yet in the human scale is the paid guardian of law and honesty and order who holds out his hand for the petty bribe to protect these itinerant grafters, and by so doing becomes the very king of grafters himself.

AN INTERPRETATION OF THE LANGUAGE OF SYMBOLS

About a quarter of a century ago there dwelt among the sand hills that bury the ancient city of Carthage a venerable Bedouin Chief, who was an Adept of the "Lesser Mysteries." Access to him was gained only by a privileged few who were called there unawares by the inexorable "Law" of past ages to receive the knowledge he had to give and reawaken memories that had long been dormant. Among the favored few was one to whom he gave great inspiration and understanding with exhortations to proceed along the path of research he described until the "Line of Light"—(of Correspondence) should be revealed between the Heavens, The Earth and Man. Moreover he averred that this "Line of Light" had long been lost to Man's external life, in the density of sense activities and that if recovered it would open the way to a higher, truer interpretation of the Truth, the Light and Life.

So following this "Line of Light" out into the Heavens we are immersed in the halo of our first Supreme Symbol—for the Universe is the Symbol of God! Everything that has form is a symbol of the desire, the will, the intelligence, the law or the motive that created it. God's worlds in space then must be the symbols of divine desire, divine will, divine intelligence, divine law and divine motive, and if we would be true to the spirit of Symbology we must first give them their rightful places. Our own planet then becomes a symbol of special significance to us, and if we seek knowledge of it through the language of symbols, there will be revealed to us the spirit, desire, will, intelligence, law and motive that created it, and we shall learn that it is one of God's children in the universal scheme of creation, possessing individuality, purpose, life and order, having character, and the differing ratios of consciousness that constitute a "living soul" full of divine inheritance—for why may not the character and soul of our planet be made up of the aggregate individual soul life upon it and in its atmosphere? And why may not all the planets of our solar system have an equal share in this divine inheritance? Students of astrology know the diverging effects produced by these planets upon our earth and human character, mythology has preserved this truth through giving to Saturn the character of the " Reaper," to Jupiter the character of the "Benefic One," to Jove the character that makes the thunder-bolt, to Mars the character of "God of War," to Mercury the character of "Messenger," to Venus the character of "Goddess of Love," etc., and an esoteric interpretation of the symbols of these planets affords sufficient evidence for the support of such an hypothesis, besides much occult knowledge confirms it. It is known there is but one Law in God's creation and if we extend that Law as it is known, from the human into its larger possibilities, we at once establish the premise of that ancient maxim "As it is above so is it below" and also "That which is true of the lesser is true of the greater" and vice versa, so following along this "Line of Light" we soon reach the realm of "First Cause" in which we may find the Spirit of all forms. Thus if we would seek the spirit of a form or symbol we must look beyond its surface, beyond that which it appears to be; we must study the law of its Being, and it is just here that the moral of our subject asserts its importance and impels one always to look beneath the surface, beyond the form, back of the symbol for the Spirit and the Life that will reveal the Soul in all things, moreover will reveal the motif in human evolvement which initiates the ratios of consciousness, that perpetuate the human Soul through Eternity. Thus it may be seen why it is in this realm alone we may find our Causes.

The failure to recognize and to conform to this simple method, has led civilizations into idolatry and slavery, nations into war and ignorance, and families into error and dissension, while it is always a sign of weakness in the individual. We dwell too much with externals, we judge too often from appearances, we need a higher education along these special lines.

Cause is ever an invisible factor, the life or spirit of a form is always with its ideal and motive, as for instance, using a common, though comprehensive illustration—If one desires to build a house, one first has an idea of the kind of house to be bulit, so the desire grows into the will; the mind is set to work and the intellect constructs the plans; the law of the arts and sciences is brought to bear upon it and the combined result shows the motive for a home. Thus is our ideal formed. An architect makes minute calculations as to the amount of lumber and materials needed, and in the invisible—in the realm of Cause—or in the "astral" as a Theosophist might put it, the house is complete; but one could not make a home of it until the thought manifests in substance.

So all things have their origin in the invisible world of Cause, and it may now become evident how "The Book of Life" exists as an actual Record of these invisible Causes, although some of them may never mature into form, for our desires, thoughts, will and design cannot be projected at any time without a record being made and this record becomes the "Law of Life" which is registered by the planets in the Zodiac for an individual incarnation, and "The Book of Life" is the Zodiac! This "Law of Life" is possible of interpretation under right conditions, and with a knowledge of the esoteric truth that underlies the whole structure of Zodiacal symbolism there is a never failing means of interpreting the "Law of Life" through the pages of the "Book." Forms and bodies are ever changing, but ideals live on forever, yet nothing could be realized on the phenomenal plan without the form. So the symbol as a manifestation of the spirit, the thought, the desire, the will and the motive, has a sacred place.

Man as a symbol is an example of the evolutionary process of nature. Man has evolved, and is a result of the increased ratios of consciousness which in their incipiency gave form to the rocks, minerals, vegetable, fish, bird and animal species. It took untold ages to form Man's body so that it might be fit to receive the "Breath of Life" and become a "Living Soul," that is, a conscious Being. Man was thus created the "Image of God" and made the conscious symbol of God's majesty and glory.

At this point in the evolution of life upon this planet, Man became a creator. Endowed with the powers of the spirit, and a consciousness which was his Soul, with a body or form through which to function, he was made an independent thinking being, responsible for his acts. Man's evolution did not cease with his reception of consciousness. Man was to evolve himself from this point of innocence, through the mazes of the physical, up into the moral, still higher into the mental, and beyond that, into the spiritual state of consciousness to become an adept, a master, a god, a Christ! How Man has accomplished this may in part be known, and an elucidation derived through the language of symbols that reveal or hide the history of his evolution through the ages. That Man has risen to great heights and fallen to great depths is recorded in the symbols he has made and left along the vistas of time. His great heights may be measured to a degree by the monuments of antiquity, by the company of stars and constellations in the heavens that eternally "declare the glory of God," together with the vast accumulation of symbols that are unmistakable evidence of, and bear witness to, man's intelligent understanding of the hidden forces of nature, of the application of attained knowledge to the arts and sciences, of their correspondence to nature, and of the necessity which impelled the mind of Man in past ages, to plan and construct these signal records for posterity. Man's knowledge of occult law, of the great cycles of time, of mathematics, geometry, astronomy and astrology—astrology possessing the very foundation and fundamental principles of wisdom—all these show a mastery and adeptship that history has not repeated. The Wise Ones, the holders of wisdom, did not build their temples and monuments then as we do now, without apparent aim or purpose, except to serve for the moment; they put into their architecture the knowledge they possessed of the hidden forces of the Universe, and formulated their religions from the essence of divine revelation as to the destiny of Man, in order that future ages might know the heights to which they had attained. For as they knew the law of cycles and planetary revolutions and the story of the Soul as it is held in the symbology of the constellations and the Sacred literatures of all peoples, they knew the depths that would follow the heights, and the rise again to other heights greater than their own. We are rising to one of those heights in our present era and that is one reason why these interpretations are possible. The depths to which Man has fallen may always be known and measured by the ignorance, the bondage, the devastation of a people or a race, and a barren waste, a desert plane, or a savage tribe is its symbol! So all these symbols may be studied as records until the knowledge and wisdom embodied in them becomes revealed and the "Line of Light" illumines the pathway.

LIFES GOALS

Life throughout the ages has been a knotty problem. Great souls, as we know, have tackled it, and have left to us their words. And yet, after all the experiences of famous prophets, mystics and philosophers, our knowledge of life's goal is rather hazy. But we may be thankful that here and there stands a seeming guide-post on our devious journey.

It has been quite universally recognized that to know God, to gain a union with Him, is the supreme aim of mankind. A seeming law of progress for the soul points to some exceedingly high and, at present, inscrutable ideal. We have Christ, and Buddha, and many other great and inspired geniuses to exhort our souls to higher and still higher planes of existence. Jesus's position, according to his own words, was, "I and my Father are one." And if we are uncompromising idealists, we too demand to be in perfect union with God.

And what course should we take to realize our desire in this? Evidently it is not the mere physical nature that is to be set to work to satisfy this longing. It is man's inner spiritual apparatus that is superior in subtle strength and acuteness to his material being, and the faculties of mind we should turn to for guidance,—to imagination, meditation, intuition and the mystic sense. God must be sought within the soul; a pure inwardness would seem to be the path along which we should endeavor to travel. It is not the objective, but the subjective sight that should be exercised to make headway toward the goal of God. This introspective activity provokes inspiration, makes conditions right for intuition, and invites revelations from the more celestial regions. It is gleams and flashes from out the psychic realm that illuminate the way. By putting our interior nature in the proper attitude the divine influences are able to reach us. By emptying the worldly slop from the mortal vessel of our being we prepare it for the inflow of the crystal waters of the higher life. We must still the boisterous activity of the brain to give us that peculiar receptivity that prepares us to receive the ever-ready favors and grace of the Over-soul, or the Omnipresent One. By opening our spiritual sluice we at the same time open the floodgate of the limitless Reservoir of Good, which is essentially the main substance of God. At least He in whom we live and have our being seems to be a kind of Principle of Good; and we should teach our souls to conform to this fundamental or divine law to realize something of a continuous advance toward the solution of the very intricate problem of life. Many theologians and mystic philosophers tell us that it is only through the grace of God—inapprehensible and searchless as He may be—that man's soul is made less and less benighted. And yet it is evident that we must exercise a sort of delicate psychic finesse in holding up the bowl to this postulated God, or the great Provider seems indifferent about filling it with the manna of life. Or the human must make his mind a tabularasa before the Omniscient One will write upon it the eternal truth.

But this relation of subject and object does not always obtain. Once the receptive soul be opened and kept so, God gradually comes into the consciousness of mortal being; or the spiritual individuality of finite man is absorbed piece-meal by the *Divine Substance*. The process is so inscrutable that it is quite impossible to tell just what does take place in this merging of humanity and Divinity, and there is only the general realization of unification. For a long time there seem to be some obscure impedimenta that keep God from coming completely into the circle of this consciousness of ours, but He does make head through the fortuitous attitudes and changes of psychical moods in our willing invitation to Him. And after a seeming thorough elimination of ourselves, as mystics tell us, He holds sway —if only for short periods—in an indescribable manner. In one interesting passage, Eckhardt, the German mystic of medieval times, says: "Whoever would see God must be dead to himself and buried in God, in the unrevealed desert Godhead, to become again what he was before he was."

This fusing, blending or absorption of the human in the Divine; and how it may be done is likely the sole and all comprehensive problem of existence. Evidently it cannot be dealt with in one sitting, since time is no doubt an ingredient to be included in the solution, as we observe that in the passing of time new light is constantly coming to us. But a prophetic view we have of a sort of transcendent future wherein God is rightfully and benevolently to usurp the reign of mortal affairs and transmute the phenomena of earth into the gold of heaven, graciously and obligingly banishing man completely from the only consciousness of life that we know anything about, and filling it Himself from the incalculably small to the immeasurably great, very likely instituting all those ideal things which man has dimly imaged as the very appropriate furniture at life's goal, and putting the stamp of immortality or deathlessness across the whole breadth of His own Immensity.

THE PHILOSOPHY OF SYMBOLISM

There may be some of our readers for whom the subject of Symbolism has not a clear meaning and for them a few words of explanation with a brief reiteration of statements made in a previous article may not prove amiss.

A symbol is any form. Back of the form—the symbol—there is something invisible, intangible, that gives character to the symbol and is its cause.

The Philosophy of Symbolism seeks to find and reveal that something, that cause, and define its relation to the form—its effect; moreover it seeks to relate that cause to the effect in such a way that it can never again be thought of as separate, but always coexistent with it. Worcester defines Symbolism as "an exposition of symbols" and "a symbol is a type, an emblem, a sign, a religious creed, a love of wisdom and knowledge." He divides Philosophy into three parts: "Natural, or that which pertains to physics; intellectual, pertaining to metaphysics; and moral, which relates to ethics."

The Philosophy of Symbolism therefore is a synthetic analysis of symbols, and with their esoteric meanings involves the love of the spirit that lies back of the symbol, and impels the research that gives knowledge and wisdom. We shall find it includes the three parts, the natural, the intellectual, and the moral; moreover, we shall find that in its application to human character and life, there is ever a guiding inspiration towards that phase of philosophy which will reveal the "Line of Light" we are seeking that exists between the heavens, the earth, and Man; hence we emphasize a previous statement that the visible universe is a symbol of God's creativeness; that every manifestation of form shows the result, the effect of a divine purpose; that our bodies are the symbols formed through the mind, the desire, the motive, the thought which constitutes the character that gives to each body its type, its outline and its personality; that everything Man has made, or is making, is the symbol of Man's creativeness.

Within the philosophy of Symbolism, therefore, character becomes a record of the spirit and design which lies back of its symbols, and as it is a record of character, so it is a record of human progress and Man's effort to perpetuate through its created forms a mystery language that underlies the whole of symbolism. The dot, horizontal and upright lines, the sphere, the circle, crescent, cross, star, square, trine, etc., are termed geometric symbols; because they demonstrate the law and sequences of forms through which Nature seeks expression and elucidate their principles through mathematics, geometry, numbers and letters. No form exists without one or more of these symbols, and Man's body includes them all. In mechanics, architecture, art and music, Man makes use of these for stability, beauty of outline, perfection of standards and endurance. These symbols will be analyzed later.

The Philosophy of Symbolism may be divided into two parts: that which pertains to natural phenomena, and that which relates to Man's creation and invention. As we look upon Nature and view her in her myriads of forms, we sense the desire of God to manifest Himself in the world of form; hence the starry dome of the heavens becomes to us the symbol of His majesty and glory; the Sun becomes the symbol of His Spirit, His Intelligence; the vast blue depths of space, the symbol of the Mother Consciousness—the "Universal Soul"; the Moon, the symbol of His Desire, and the earth, the trees, the waters, the mountains and the valleys, the rocks and creeping things, the birds, the animals, the flowers, are seen as the symbols of His Will, His Ideals, His Power and His Love for creation; while Man in his turn becomes the symbol of God's divinity. All that Man has done therefore becomes the symbol of the same desire to manifest himself in form. His desire to perpetuate himself in architecture, in art, in sculpture, in fabrics, in music and invention, originates in the Divine Desire to perpetuate itself through the human. So Man builds houses, makes implements with which to fashion his designs, invents machines, commands the elements (outside and within himself), erects monuments, and each age and civilization bears the mark of the wisdom and knowledge to which Man has attained. When the cycles return to bring Man into recognition of his greater consciousness and reveal to him the mysteries and meanings of his own creations, they are recalled from the memories of the sub-conscious mind and are so revealed to him.

The ancient systems of Symbolism extend far back into the ages. We find them in the religion, science and philosophy of the Jewish Kabbalah, in the hymns of the Vedas; in the philosophies that grew out of, and were perpetuated by the teachings of Confucius, Lao-tzu, Buddha, Zoroaster and Mohammed, by the schools of Alexandria and Luxor; by Pythagoras, Plato, Jesus and the Persian Magi, and the records of the wisdom they taught no modern school can yet approach. It is with the hope to make a beginning in the revival of some of the knowledge leading towards the "Lesser Mysteries" and to show wherein is hidden the law of requirement for an approach to the "Greater Mysteries" that this series of articles has been formulated. The religion, science and philosophies these ancient peoples sought to perpetuate through their literatures are also hidden in various monuments of antiquity which give character to the symbols that preserve them and reveal that they were built or established for a definite purpose at the crests of the waves of civilization that marked their epochs.

It was mentioned in a previous article that these monuments reveal a profound understanding of the laws of physics, mathematics, chemistry, alchemy, astronomy and astrology; moreover some of them demonstrate that they were built with a complete knowledge of planetary revolutions, declinations and right ascensions.

The temples and pyramids of Egypt, the Sphinx, the Ziggurats of Chaldea, the temples of Persia, India, China and Japan; the colossal statue of Buddha and of Memnon, the temples of Central America and Yucatan and of Peru, even the prehistoric ruins of temples in the United States, each in its way shows a part of this universal philosophy and are the symbols which preserve it. The Pyramids of Egypt show the technical precision it was necessary to establish at that degree of civilization and reveal the highest conception of science, geometry and mathematics.

The Ziggurats of Chaldea combine the beauty of outline and rare coloring in contrast to the stern cut angles and cold greyness of the Pyramids and reveal an unquestionable insight into vibratory law as expressed in colors, tones, letters and numbers. They were each built upon a square, the Pyramids with four trines, the Ziggurats in tiers of three, five and seven, all sacred numbers relating to the manifestation of an inner comprehension of the laws involved. Each tier of the Ziggurats represents planetary effects in color and tone winch are preserved even to this day in exquisite tints, showing a profound knowledge of the principles for which the planets stand and their relations to Man in their correspondences.

The colossal statues of the Buddha and Memnon unite the masculine technicalities of the Pyramids and the charm of feminine dignity of the Ziggurats in the human form and these monuments are the symbols of science, philosophy and religion, through which may be traced a history of the cosmogony of the world, the involution of the Spirit of God and the evolution of Consciousness through the human soul to its final destiny in the Godhead.

Pyramid means a mound, or mountain to Fire, in other words to the Sun, an "Altar to the Lord of Hosts in the midst of the land of Syria!" The accompanying chart is an illustration of some of the mysteries revealed by an esoteric insight into the Pyramids. It reveals the fact that the Pyramids were designed and built upon a plan that corresponds to our solar system.

The zodiacal circle (Fig 1) touches the points of the square of its base; the four trines of its sides are the symbols of the four elements and include what is known in Astrology as the four "triplicities," there being three signs of earth, three of fire, three of water and three of air. The orbits of the planets are in ratio to their distances from the Sun. The inner points of the five pointed star touch the orbit of the earth and reveal to the esoteric student that earth life is destined to fulfill a mission in the divine economy of our solar system; that through the symbology of this human symbol Man is shown how he is to aid the fulfilment of this mission, how through his own conscious effort he is to

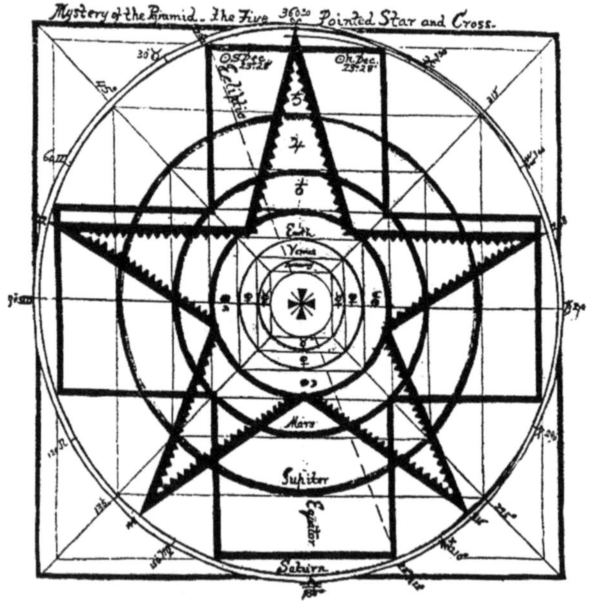

Fig. 1

gain that self-control and mastery of natural forces that will enable him to transmute the five physical senses into their higher potentialities of godliness, holiness and love, and thus raise the ratio of consciousness for the planet. Jesus the Christ was the example for this process and completion of destiny; His character, life and "miracles" are evidence of the extent to which the human race is privileged, for the example given by Jesus consummates the fulfilment of the Law of Love and shows the probable ultimate destiny of the human race upon the planet earth. The five-pointed star is a symbol of generate and re-generate Man—of Man coming to the knowledge of his divine self, through his own volition. No wonder then that the "Wise Men" of two thousand years ago looked for a "star in the east" that was to herald the advent of that consciously redeemed Soul destined to light the pathway to Man's redemption. Five is what is termed a pivotal number, that is, a number having two dualities, two inclusions of masculine and feminine principles, with a pivot to unite them; the pivot is always the spiritual potentiality; the dualities signify that the masculine and feminine elements individualized through repeated manifestations of the human soul upon earth as separate entities, have become unified and perfected in one. The five-pointed star, always a symbol of promise, is the cosmic emblem of the man Jesus, who was subject to Nature's law—the "Son of Man" that was to reveal the "Son of

God" and show the way to regeneration. The beautiful symbolism of the five-pointed "wonder star" is further elucidated by the fact that it is evolved from the angle of 72 degrees which relates to the full number of the Sacred Name—Jehovah! the Creator.

MANS INNER GUIDES

The era of emancipation from the thralldom of woeful worship is dawning. Man is no longer content with man-made creeds. His heart cries out for freedom. He feels something stirring within his being, something akin to what he has been taught to look upon as a far-away Ruler of Righteousness; indeed, a Supreme Ruler of earth and sky whose nature is Divine, though at times vindictive, violently provoked, and furiously inclined. By the application of common-sense man has learned to discriminate between false teachings and true knowledge. He is no longer held in bondage by the voice of fear. He feels surer of himself on matters of deeper importance for the welfare of his complex being. And, though his thoughts clash with the antiquated beliefs of priest and prince, his better judgment tells him not to worry about what these self-styled rulers of men declare they will do to him if he dares to laugh, to scorn their Decalogue's of rotting rules of conduct and testaments of over-inflated and tyrannical catechisms of obedience.

These welcome signs of individual awakening point to a further realization on man's part that what others have done in the past and are doing in the present, he can also do. If the Great Law of impartial justice still operates with mathematical precision for beast and man, then, truly, nothing is impossible of achievement and no Power is too sacred to be totally ignored for fear of incurring the ill-will of a 'touch-me-not' potentate.

Thus it is that man reasons and speculates on the possibilities and hidden potencies of his heretofore neglected better nature. He has chosen to burn midnight oil for the explicit purpose of finding out for himself whether the promptings of the heart are of more value to him in the actual living of a life of peace than are the unreasonable requests of a veritable host of greedy and dominant impostors.

As a direct result of this novel attitude of mind toward things that were usually taken as a matter of course, because of an existing belief that regal mantle and cap-and-gown were the only duly assigned administrators of Godly justice, man has risen above the level of vicarious service, and, by crawling out of his limited shell of physical dependence with his eyes open to the Light of Truth that is streaming through his soul, he has reached the plane of a higher understanding and resolved to do his own thinking, come what may!

This resolution has transformed the mortal man of flesh and bones into a creature of renascent Reality. It has made of him a Son of God in the making. It has given him the strength to overcome the evils in his own nature and align himself with the constructive forces for the greatest good of down-trodden and deceived mankind. The words of Pope ring true in his ears because they voice a sentiment of a high caliber and comforting hope: "Man, know then thyself, presume not God to scan; the proper study of mankind is man."

Man is literally letting "the dead past bury its dead." He has given up worrying about the final outcome of life. His better nature tells him that all is well with the world and all the world is watching and waiting for the coming of the Son of God that has come to life within him.

Realizing this for the first time in his life, this Son of God within man has virtually and truly become a tangible asset to man and through man is gradually unfolding the secrets of all the ages past; placing as it were the Keys of the mysteries of being within his ready reach and impelling him to search the depths of his own nature for the priceless heritage of enduring riches. The peculiar inner urge that men felt now and then has become a vivid sense of conscious awareness. And the thing called conscience is no longer a bugaboo of terror but is, instead of this, a voice of lovable and delightful helpfulness, a Great Friend in the hour of need, and a constant companion possessing prestige and Power, plus the courage to do things in accordance with those standards of conduct which are the visible symbols of an all-knowing Inner Guide. And thus vagary, vacuity and vacillation of mind have been superseded by the holy trinity of intuitive conviction, divine inspiration, and steadiness of aim in the quest of wisdom.

High-sounding titles are no longer necessary to place man in touch with the Reality within his being. Education is to be desired and striven for with determination of purpose and singleness of aim. But it does not really matter whether man has matriculated from the ranks of nobility or from the files of earthly limitations. If his heart is pure and his mind free from bias he will be received with open arms by the teachers of mankind and be dealt with impartial good-will and loving interest in whatsoever channel he may choose to sail. No one will be able to thwart his plans. No one will succeed in weaning him away from his ideal. Likewise, having his whole nature attuned to unselfish love he will render a creditable account of himself ere his Inner Guide calls him to other labors. With his mind centered on the up-liftment of the race and his thoughts trained to respond to the call of the directive Will within him, he will soon soar to the heights beyond the commonplace and, casting a loving glance over the panorama that greets his new-born sight, he will gladly forget his passion for place and pledge the best part of his nature to the *Great Cause* of *Truth*.

To such an one pleasure is hidden in service and happiness is extracted from the perplexing and puzzling duties of the day. Being free to function on many planes of human need with consciousness aroused and the will set for any trial or care, this resurrected being strikes out in boldest fashion for the hilltops of superior achievement and synthesized virtue. He knows the cost of sorrow because he has experienced it. He knows the price of selfishness because he himself was formerly selfish. And now that he understands the purpose of the Plan that his Inner Guide laid out in the beginning he is ready to bear every trial and share every sort of joy found by the way-side of life. Having passed through the refining fire of personal experience and burned off the ragged edges of his selfish nature of his own free will and accord he is now glad to tell the world something about man's true relationship to his Inner Guide and to the Invisible Intelligence that causes him to live and move and have his being on earth.

The sublime sentinel guarding the fort of man's heart is none other than his Inner Guide. This is the meaning of Reality. Man's Real Self stands for It. The *True God* of man's being is the *Divine Voice* rooted in the core of his inner nature. This living and loving Reality is in man to inspire and assist him whenever there is need. Man can, if he so chooses, manifest the presence of his Inner Guide, this God within him, to the world about him. He has it within his Power to grow more and more like Him and not only reflect the *Divine Image* and Likeness of his indwelling Master, but, too, he can become a living counter-part of all that his Inner Guide stands for; that is: Love, Light, *Divinity, Wisdom, Understanding, Truth, Honor, Courage, Youth, Freedom,* and the countless and numberless other characteristics that voice the immanence of God in man's being.

What the God in man is, man can become. What man's Inner God stands for, man can translate into action while yet in the body of flesh. He does this by a resolute firmness of mind. And, by growing like his Inner Guide, the True God of his soul, he conquers every foe, overcomes every obstacle in his path, and meets every lion on the way face to face with a coolness that bespeaks superiority of knowledge and supremacy of intuitive conviction. Even death has no terror for him. He knows that death is but a talisman of a new and better beginning with friends and loving companions in receptive attitude of mind and welcoming preparation of soul. Through his schooling he has learned to smile upon the Great Reaper when the hour of his emancipation from physical embodiment strikes. His training has enabled him to raise his action to the higher level of conscious unification with his indwelling Guide; the

Christ-Power within his being. It is man's Inner Guide that cries out for freedom. It is this Voice that speaks in the silence of man's soul with the courage that is born of conviction. This is the Presence that says:

I am resolved!—No autocrat, or despot, shall coerce My liberty.
No tyrant, nor dominant ruler shall claim My freedom.
No vile wielder of bloody weapons shall break My God-like will.
These gifts are mine!—to use with judgment and discretion,
For the greatest good of impoverished and enslaved humanity.

Again, and with like force, the *Real Self* sings Its song of freedom on the Altar of Independence.

Realizing that all-Power is his to use He summons every atom of activity to the fore and with new-born eloquence registers Its pledge of honor on the sensitive plate of universal permanence. His first and foremost promise is: "I will serve and do my best." And then the Voice of invincible definiteness gives form to the Inner Guide's code of confidence thus:

OPPORTUNITY: O Port of Unity O Port of Unity:

"I" recognize, The force that Power of Will now dares capsize.
And that the Central Eye of mind and brain,
Fears neither fate nor chance; nor fire nor rain. But works and waits secure upon its throne, And with steadfast calm starves the worthless drone;
That leans on limbs of straw and walks on sand,
The blindest bully on this mighty land:
Of wealth and opportunities galore;
A land enriched by things that men adore. Filled from base to brim with the golden grain, That man produces with his Inner brain;
When once awakened by the might and Power Of soul, confined in mind's creative tower. Wherein dwells the Spirit that controls,
And gives direction to all living souls

O Port of Unity: "I" will to solve,

The deeper problems that my eyes convolve.
In bold attempts to twist my soul in brain.
Into a shapeless mass of thoughts that drain
My heart, of love, and cause my will to

swerve, From the chosen course that mankind would serve.
To bring to naught my one selected
Goal,
And cause my Self to drift on arid shoal.
Until the Spark of Life shall hope no more,
To earn its passage to the fairer shore.
Where neither time, nor tide control the day,
Nor mortal shams the hands of
Justice stay.
A Kingdom that is ruled by right and light,
Instead of carnal lusts that fight to fright.
In selfish hopes hidden in a weazen brain;
That righteous complement that weak minds contain

O Port of Unity: "I" now resolve,
To live my life so that I may absolve
My Inner Self from thoughts that have been lame,
And nev'r again refill my heart with shame.
The shame that's heaped through ignorance of truth,
Upon the plastic brow of care-free youth; As well as on the heads of sinners old,
Who paid no heed to what their "I" had told:
With pangs of bitter pain and stress of sin,
And through the warnings of their kith and kin. Seeking to enlighten a shiftless mind,
By pointing out the Path that men must find.
In the central midst of a dried-up brain,

Whose "Jewel" in the heat of strife has lain;
Until its priceless grandeur has been lost,
And petty man has had to pay the cost.

Opportunity; O Port of Unity.

You and "I" are One; Let US now live and love and serve until our work is done!

From the above it is evident that man must become more than man before it is possible for him to get in tune with his Inner Guide, or Real Self, or God. His first cue is to understand that man is not Real until he finds out what that 'Something' is that makes him a man. That in order to manifest the *God-Presence* he must possess the *Power* to *Dare* assert his individuality; meaning, of course, his inner convictions. He must know whereof he speaks. He must possess the *Courage* to *Do* the things he knows he ought to do, at all times and places, under all circumstances and conditions. Moreover, he must possess the disposition to *Keep Silent* in order to protect the interests of humanity and add moral force to the Spirit of the Age in which he lives.

Man must learn that manifestation is but retardation of motion. This definition lifts the veil from the mystery of creation by interpreting for man the essential meaning of the Biblical statement: "Before Abraham was, I AM." (Let not him that seeketh cease from his search until he finds.) Verily, then, an ideal conception is but an arrested Reality. Substance is immanent in matter though its vibratory rate of motion is walled in and lies latent until the outer gets in tune with the Inner and establishes unity of natures. At the point of balance a harmonic relationship nullifies the resistance exerted over the indwelling Reality and allows the Substance to leap forth to freedom.

Therefore, that which has been manifested may be easily and readily reproduced, but that which is ideal defies the brain and skill of him who possesses no Key to its invisible potentiality. The logical deduction is self-evident.

And anyone possessed of normal intelligence will agree that: *It is not hard to do something when another has pointed out the way, but the worth of a man lies in his ability to **initiate** that which is latent in the secrecy of his being and in the universe about and around, under and over him; leaving to other less-gifted mortals the mockery of imitation and the shallow* *consolation derived from a covetous sense of profiting through the initiative power of the creator's superior brain: man's Inner Guide.*

THE DANGERS AND VALUE OF HABIT

So sure a seconder to desire is habit, that to ignore its power would be either to close our eyes to the presence of a most subtle foe or to refuse the service of a most potent ally.

Habit, than which no more relentless executioner can be found if we have fixed it in such practices as belong to the destructive aspects of desire, becomes a ministering angel in our struggle towards reconstruction; more, it becomes a staff by the support of which we may pass safely over many a quagmire of difficulty and climb many a height of attainment.

Who does not admit, from observation, if no more, how irresistible is the drive of evil habits of mind or body? Drunkenness, drugs, license; all recognize the power of these to possess and the difficulty in overcoming them, once their hold has become fixed. Nor are these the only deadly enemies which may be fostered to our ultimate undoing. Pernicious bents of mind, sullenness, revenge, hatred, indolence and a host of others go to swell the ranks of habits to be shunned if threatening, and conquered if they have gained a foothold. It should not be difficult, therefore, to realize readily how important, how helpful, how tremendous may become the assistance of habit, once we draft it in the service of high ideals and noble purpose.

Established religions recognize the value of this force as one of the potent factors in redemption; psychology acclaims its usefulness, medical science recommends habits of regularity of life and cleanliness of body. Devotees of all religions set apart certain regular times for prayer, meditation, alms giving. Why? *Because repetition of an act at set times and regular intervals tends to establish automatic recurrence of that act*. In mental and moral philosophy alike, this is axiomatic.

We find Saint Thomas A'Kempis saying, "For first there cometh to the mind a bare thought of evil, then a strong imagination thereof, afterwards delight, and evil motion, and then consent." He should have added that consent breeds habit.

By substituting for "evil" good, aspiration, the Ideal, God, or the DIVINE SELF, the process of development is identical.

Through habit, hunger asserts itself at stated hours; to assure waking from sleep at a given time daily, is not difficult to accomplish; indeed, it is a very common form of suggestion. Autosuggestion? Certainly; but all impulses are more or less due to auto-suggestion. There is nothing wrong in it *per se*; it is only desire vivified and made active through the image making faculty, supplemented by directing will.

In schools of occultism as in exoteric religions, to establish certain habits is one of the first exercises enjoined upon the aspirant because, once established, the habit will assert itself automatically, demanding recognition and compliance, over-riding momentary preoccupation, indolence and other interests; soul, mind and body will respond to the prompting instantly and in mutual accord, thus assuring attunement of the whole man at the designated moment and at the desired interval.

Posture is another important factor. So close is the sympathy between known states of mind or emotion and bodily posture, that in art and the drama certain poses symbolize states of the inner man because almost universally, under the pressure of those states, men naturally fall into the sympathetic attitude. As for example, “Il Penseroso” by Michael Angelo and “The Thinker” by Rodin. Anyone glancing at these figures without knowing the titles affixed to them would immediately grasp that they represent thinking; so universally is that particular pose associated with the process of pondering or intense thought.

An angry child will clench his fists instinctively, though he knows nothing of pugilism. Anger or indignation prompt the body to assume an aggressive or defensive attitude. In fact, it is possible to induce deep thinking by assuming an attitude corresponding to it, and aggressiveness may be aroused by clenching the hands with the idea of injury present in the consciousness. Thus, definite posture in conjunction with a habit of mind work together to a common end.

For example; if meditation at a certain hour is to be established, a posture consonant with that exercise should be chosen. Strict adherence to the order laid down will, before long, fix automatic recurrence of both the posture and the mental state. Without clock or other signal, as the appointed moment approaches the man will find his whole being falling naturally into the meditative state, while his body will assume the posture without direct effort on his part, to so place it.

Inversely, so intimate does this correlation between the mind and its vehicle eventually become, that assumption of the prescribed posture will react automatically upon the mind and rouse those ideas, conceptions, aspirations or desires which are the objects of his meditation.

How valuable is the aid thus rendered must be evident, for, with such automatic recurrences established, the mind and body alike are left free to perform other necessary acts with undivided attention and, undivided attention to the matter in hand, whatever it may be, is a *sine qua non* of bringing it to satisfactory fruition. Scattered thoughts and acts bear but poor fruit.

All things, all tendencies, all potentialities are for our use. That we have perverted them in our ignorance and clothed them in the semblance of obsessing demons does not make them inherently such; we can and should convert them into angels of light which shall mightily abet us in our journey upon the path of Wisdom, Beauty and Truth.

LESSON IN HIGHER KNOWLEDGE

History shows us that the greatest thinkers in antiquity received their knowledge by initiation into the mysteries of Egypt, India and elsewhere. This science studied by the most profound philosophers, of their time is known under various names—Occult Science, Magic, Hermetism, Occultism, Esoterism, etc.: identical in its principles, one code of instructions constitutes this great science which is most generally known under the' name of occultism. This science embraces the theory and practice of a vast amount, of phenomena, a small part of which at the present time comes under the domain of magnetism and the evocation of spirits. In fact, the teachings of the present time, save in rare exceptions, form but a small part of this grand science which comprehends three grand divisions: Theurgy, Magic, Alchemy.

The study of occultism may be considered from two points of view. One may follow the formulae of the ancient masters, or may follow out a line of experimental work with the secret laws of the universe which are but little known at present.

There is too great a tendency to confound the science with the sciences.

The former is immutable in its principles, and the latter varies according to the caprices of men. As occult science may be correctly termed the eternal truth.

But without investigation and with preconceived ideas the skeptic asks—Can you find any trace of this pretended science of the Ancients? What is the secret knowledge? And how can one learn the famous science of which you speak?

In dignified silence we may point to the old monuments of the Orient, to symbols, hieroglyphics, the diverse rites of initiation, and many sacred manuscripts which have been preserved through the lapse of centuries.

But all of these are unintelligible and undecipherable without the key. It is this latter which all are anxious to possess.

As a solid basis for this knowledge we may begin with the School of Alexandria, Pythagoras, Plato. Aristotle, Pliny and many others.

It is not by any means an easy task to reconstruct these ancient writings so as to make them presentable to the nineteenth century student. In Astronomy the ancients knew that the earth revolved around the sun. The theory of a plurality of worlds, universal attraction, that tides were the result of lunar attraction, the constitution of the milky way, and above all they were familiar with the laws rediscovered by Newton.

Plutarch was familiar with nearly all the brilliant truths of Astronomy, and also discovered the law of reciprocity by which the planets acted one upon the other.

It is claimed that the greater part of the Egyptian mysteries was but a veil to cover the practical sciences, and that initiation into their mysteries was no more than the study of known sciences. But we find that they called the planet Jupiter the Elicius, or Jupiter the Electrical, which plainly shows that they were cognizant of the attractive power of this immense world. In Chapter IV, "The Mission of the Jews," we find the following:

"The manuscripts of Athos and Pauselenus show that the ancient *Ioian* authors understood the application of chemical photography, the dark chamber, optical apparatus, metallic sensitive plates, etc.," as was later developed by Daguerre.

Thus we have reason to believe the ancients developed the science of chemistry from their alchemical researches and possessed superior knowledge of its theory and practice than do our modern chemists of today.

The student must bear in mind that many alleged discoveries of modern times were old and well-known facts to the ancients. Science with the ancients was secret or esoteric.

Whereas the science of the moderns is the study of the visible or exoteric.

After having determined that the ancients gave more attention to the workings of nature's secret laws, we shall endeavor to analyze some, of the methods employed.

They sought to understand the invisible by a study of the visible and the unreal by a study of the real.

The first question to be determined is whether or not a relation exists between the visible and the invisible, or if the idea is simply a mystical expression.

The principal method employed in the past was analogy.

By analogy we are able to determine the relations existing between phenomena. As in all efforts to understand the Higher or more profound mysteries we must begin with the study of Mem.

As man is the archetype and contains within himself a reflection of all laws in the Universe. It was for this reason the ancients called man the microcosm, or little world, while to the universe they gave the name of macrocosm, or great world.

One may begin by a study of the organs and their function; this is called study of the visible by induction.

One may study man by his life, or intelligence, or what some call soul. This is the study of the invisible by deduction.

Or we may unite the two methods by considering the relations existing between the organs and their functions or between two organs and two functions. This is study by analogy.

Thus, if we observe the lungs in detail we find that they receive air which enters them and undergoes certain change. If we consider the stomach in the same manner we find that it also changes the aliments which are received from without.

The science of phenomena rests here; it cannot proceed farther than known facts. We have now two organs, both of which receive something from without which undergoes a change within. Thus, the stomach and the lungs exercise functions analogous.

Continuing, we will find analogy perfectly established between the arm and the leg, the hand and the foot. We have chosen for example the analogy of the lungs and stomach to correct a very common error that two things analogous are necessarily similar.

This is a false idea, as two things may be perfectly analogous and yet not more similar than the lungs and stomach, or the hand and the foot.

The method of analogy is neither deduction nor induction, but is this light which springs from the union of the two methods. If you will walk around a monument and study even the smallest details, you will then know the relations existing between the most insignificant parts, but even so, you may not have a thorough knowledge of the ensemble.

This is called induction. If, on the other hand, you made no minute examination but climbed to the top and looked the monument over from this vantage you would have a general idea of the structure.

This is called deduction. Either of the two methods would be faulty. The real knowledge in regard to the monument will come from a union of both methods. In the same manner the metaphysician treats the mind of a patient without regard to his physical body.

While the regular practitioner treats the body without regard to the mind. The true physician will take into consideration both the mind and the body.

It will be seen as we progress in our studies in analogy that a great quantity of facts are governed by a very small number of laws. It is the study of these laws, under the, name of secondary causes, which forms the basis of science.

But these secondary causes are themselves governed by what may be termed the primary causes. The study of these latter are ignored by contemporaneous science as they can only be understood by means of a sensitive spirit.

GRADATION. We now have to begin with: First.—The domain of absolute facts. Second.—The domain of law or Secondary causes. Third.—The domain of principles, or primary causes. This gradation, based upon the number three, plays a most important role in the science of the ancients. It is upon this, that analogy has been in a great measure founded. Thus, to continue with its development, we find in man the three divisions of Body, Life and The Will.

Any part of the body, whatsoever, a finger, for example may escape control of the will without ceasing to live (as in radial or cubital paralysis).

Or it may cease to live without losing the power of motion. Here we have three distinct domains, of body and of life exerting influence through a series of special conductors, the grand sympathetic and the vasomotor nerves.

The domain of the will acts through special conductors known as the voluntary nerves. Law.—If one thing is analogous to another all the parts of that thing are analogous to the parts of the other.

Therefore, the ancients having learned that man was analogous to the universe, they reasoned that to understand the circulation of life in the universe it was sufficient to study the vital circulation of man. And to know the details concerning the birth, growth and death of man it sufficed to study the same phenomena in a world.

These statements may seem obscure to some, and mystic to others, but our readers and sincere students will find in succeeding lessons that all tends to an explanation which is absolutely necessary to the student of the occult.

TRUE OCCULTISM

Mankind as well as all things material are subject to continued change. The panoramic changes of youth, maturity, and old age are constantly before us.

The children of yesterday become the men and women of tomorrow. The seeds of springtime appear the matured grains of Autumn. Thus the enumeration might be prolonged indefinitely.

Yet we are told that neither a drop of water nor a grain of sand is ever lost. The former may change from ice to water and vice versa, or it may change to vaporous clouds, yet it will in due time return to earth again, and whether it comes in the form of snow or rain is no consequence.

Thus the material world has been called the plane of illusion because everything is, yet is not. It requires but a casual observation to note that these changes are not the result of chance but the inexorable effects of existent causes.

A further consideration will also show that many phenomena are controlled by a very few laws. A beautiful rose may bloom in the garden, showing us thereby a work of art from the great storehouse of nature which cannot be duplicated by all the science and skill of man. Yet a small boy who neither under stands its nature nor appreciates its beauty can pluck and destroy it in a moment.

A young man may return from college the pride of his family and friends with an apparently bright future before him. Yet in a few days may be stricken down by accident or disease and claimed by death without a moment's warning, causing us to doubt the generally received axiom of "The survival of the fittest."

Amid all this creation and destruction, this coming into life and passing out, the question comes to one: Why was I created? Like the small boy of a humorous play who is made to say: "What is the use of anything?"

Then laconically answers the question himself by replying: "Nothing." It is this confusion and uncertainty which accounts in a measure for the increasing number of suicides. As in an age of materialism when the hope of a future life is shaken in the minds of many, they consider that life on earth alone is hardly a just compensation for the ills and misfortunes that beset so many. But is this life all? The object of this little talk is to give a few of our reasons for firmly believing in a life beyond. Amid all of the changes before enumerated there is a cherished hope of a future life. As long as the human heart pulsates with that beautiful sensation of love just so long shall humanity extend forth its arms and look beyond the grave into that unknown realm wherein it hopes to again meet its loved ones. It is this hope of a future life which spurs mankind onward and brings out all that is good, noble and brave in nature. The thought is so truly beautiful that all wish to believe it. However, when we seek to know things beyond the veil to contemplate Infinity with our finite minds it is hardly strange if we become confused. Yet neither our hopes nor doubts can change the unyielding laws that rule all things. This being an admitted fact it behooves us to learn the law and live according to its mandates. If the question was pro pounded to a hundred persons—Do you believe in a future state of being? The answer would depend upon their early training and the maturer thoughts of later life. In a Christian community the majority would answer yes. And even among savage tribes it would be difficult to find many who do not believe in some form of a future existence. Yet if you called together one hundred scientists, men whose lives are devoted to seeking and classifying facts, we could not be so certain of their reply. Like Herbert Spencer many would say: We have seen no proof of it, therefore cannot accept it.

History, both sacred and profane, is rich with traditions concerning man's future state, as it is with regard to other questions, among which we may consider the age of the earth. Tradition, together with the story of Genesis, leads us to believe the earth is about six thousand years old. If you consult the geologist upon the same subject he will look grave and no doubt tell you that this planet must have existed mil lions of years, as he discourses upon formation epochs, periods, etc. Thus we have at present a great obstacle in the variance of tradition and science. When the higher science which embraces man, his principles and the universe, is able to command the respect of the professors in our colleges who in the present day wield so great an influence over the people, we may then hope to see educated ignorance give place to real knowledge. Each generation thinks itself wiser than its predecessor. And we do not doubt that this present age of material ism may be remembered as the reign of darkness.

During all ages of which we have any authentic record there have lived individuals or societies who have claimed the key to man's future state and to have that while still in the flesh the secret knowledge by which they could communicate with extraneous forces, entities or, beings. However, the world has always had an aversion for that which it fears. Therefore such men as Cagliostro, Paracelsus and others held an honorable place as martyrs in the hearts of those who can comprehend their true worth. Occultism is the science which treats of nature's hidden laws. And it is knowledge of the secret laws which gives us understanding, which must be the forerunner of conscious awakening. The Occult Scientist is one who can avail himself of the unseen forces which respond only to the strong will directed by knowledge. When one perverts such superhuman power he becomes a sorcerer if a man, and a sorceress if a woman.

All power which transcends the sphere of physical manifestations may be justly termed Occult. Some deny the existence of all things occult, but he who denies the possibility of occult manifestations must deny the Bible, as in it we are told that Moses performed feats of magic in the presence of Pharaoh. Saul consulted the Witch of Endor and finally Christ stands forth as the most worthy of all occultists, although not aware of it.

There are many who pass through life hungering for occult knowledge. The inner consciousness prompts them to an awakening; to a development in fact of their God-given powers. Occultism does not in any way conflict with the Bible; on the other hand this worthy book abounds in hidden truths.

Healing by the finer forces of nature may also be classed as occult phenomena. As an answer to those who decry drugless healing we have only to point to the works of Christ.

Though we are not in perfect harmony with those who in the present day claim to heal in his name. As they deny the most important factor in the work which is—suggestion. The Nazarene was not too proud to consider it a part of his duty to care for the body as well as the Spirit of his followers,—an example that might be well followed by preachers and priests of the present time; in fact everyone who lives right, thinks right and speaks right, as the Hindus say has within him the power of assuaging or curing the ills of others.

From an occult point of view healing the body is not the most important consideration. To begin with one should learn all about the material body, then investigate astral phenomena, including the astral body, then finally you will find a most interesting field in the study of the Soul or Divine body. This research, if properly conducted, will bring us to the consideration of the God within man, as it exists in all creation.

These great truths are everlasting and eternal in their status. Therefore when anyone claims to be the inventor of any of the above branches of knowledge we may with cause distrust him. Such claims remind me of a quack doctor whom I once met. After a deep breath, suggestive of his own importance, he said: “Doctor, I have been working for a long time to discover something which will remove freckles.” His time could have been otherwise employed had he known that many lotions are known to all physicians which will accomplish that end.

Thus we can refer all alleged discoverers in the fields of occultism to the lore of the Orient, as well as to the Bible. For in both the student will find the great hid den truths. Some of which have been revealed from God directly, others have been obtained through the practices of Ceremonial Magic. Apropos of the last statement we will state that a difference exists between Magic and Occult Science.

A man may be either a Magician and an Occultist—or he may be either. There are many who study and practice occultism for self-improvement, and the protection it affords. Some of whom would not under any circumstances undertake a work of Ceremonial Magic. The latter is divided into two classes—white and black. The former embraces all occult phenomena induced by action of the hidden laws directed by a pure mind, with the desire of doing good. Black magic emanates from a perverse will and is the use, of secret force for some selfish or unholy end.

This secret force is generally conceded to be the elementals which obey a strong and determined will acting under proper conditions, whether the object be good or bad.

Yet all must be aware of using such power for evil purposes, as such efforts are not free from danger. For this reason occult science has remained secret. A great responsibility rests upon him who places such power or knowledge within the reach of those who would abuse it.

Therefore the path of one who seeks to study this science is not a broad, straight highway; the path is a narrow and tortuous one. Many hundred books with alluring names are sometimes perused with but few ideas to reward the aspirant, but let not such things discourage you. If worthy and persistent, you will in due time receive your own.

SECOND LESSON IN THE HIGHER KNOWLEDGE

However, as it is necessary to prove our assertions step by step as we advance, it is well to consider two citations.

One in regard to the three hierarchies—Facts, Laws and Principles, expressed by the ancients under the name The Three Worlds. The other of the microcosm and macrocosm which is demonstrated by the doctrine of Pythagoras. The application of the number 12 to the universe is not by any means an arbitrary invention of Pythagoras, as it was common to the Chaldeans and Egyptians from whom he received it; it was also known to the leading races of the ancient world.

It was used until the division of the zodiac into twelve asterisms. But tradition shows the use of the number 12 as representing the universe from time immemorial. The distinction of the three worlds and their development into a greater or less number of concentric spheres, inhabited by intelligences pf variable purity, was not only known to Pythagoras, but was recognized at Memphis and at Babylon, and previous to this time they had received it from India.

This great Greek philosopher recognized in man throe great principles which caused him to apply the name microcosm, or little world. It was common with the ancient philosophers to com pare the universe to a great man and a great man to a; small universe. The universe was considered as a grand living creation composed of intelligence, soul and body and was called by the ancients Pan or Phanes.

Man or the microcosm is composed of the same, but in an inverse manner the body, the soul and the intelligence. And each of these three divisions may be in its, turn divided into three parts or modifications as the ternary reigns throughout all. It will be found to embrace the small divisions as well as the great. The ternary may embrace infinity just as well as it can apply, to the most insignificant individual. And each ternary comprises a unity which thus makes the quaternary.

This quaternary may be either universal or particular. This doctrine was known long before the time of Pythagoras, as it is found expressed among the records of the Chinese as well as the ancient Scandinavians. It is found elegantly expressed in the oracles of Zoroaster: *"Le Temaire partout brille dan l'Univers, Et la Monade est son principe."*

Thus, following this doctrine, man considered as a relative unity is contained in the absolute unity of the Infinite as the universal Ternary under the three principal modifications of the body, soul and spirit or intelligence. The soul is that which contains the passions. It may be expressed according to its three faculties—the reasonable or rational soul; the unreasonable soul and the soul of desire or appetite. The vices of the latter are said to be intemperance or avarice. The vice of the unreasonable soul is said to be cowardice, and that of the reasonable soul is folly. The greatest of all vices, according to the ancients, was injustice.

To avoid these, faults the philosophers recommended four principles of virtue to their disciples: Temperance to conquer the faculty of appetite, courage for the unreasonable faculty, prudence for the reasonable faculty, and for the three vices combined justice was regarded as the most perfect virtue of the soul. We have thus far considered the two numbers, twelve and three, but as numbers had for the ancients an esoteric or secret meaning, which is also important to the student who would comprehend the occult science, we shall devote some time to the esotercism of numbers.

First one may ask, whence comes this number three which fills so important a place in the writings of the ancients.

This number, which extends through their metaphysics, and comes to us throughout the centuries and is finally considered or treated by one of the world's greatest writers—Balzac.

We must first recognize the fact that the ancients employed a special language with which to record their occult knowledge. This language is now almost entirely lost. It was the language of numbers. Plato, who found in music other things from those known to the musicians of our day, found also in numbers a sense or meaning unknown to our algebraists.

To prove this mysticism of numbers it is only necessary to open any ancient book of occultism. You will find this idea reigning throughout. Note-The ancient priests had three methods of expressing their thoughts.

The first was plain and simple; the second was by the symbolism of figures; the third by the sacred hieroglyphics.

Thus they used three kinds of characters, but not three different dialects, as was generally supposed. The ancient magi having observed equilibrium in physics, concluded naturally that there must be an equilibrium in metaphysics.

Thus they recognized God as living and active and the negative upon which he acted was called matter. Therefore in the beginning they placed spirit and matter, or the movement and the stability. They recognized also the existence of three worlds—the natural, the spiritual and the divine. Therefore there must necessarily exist a cult material, a cult spiritual and a cult divine, which may be expressed by actions, words and prayers.

Although we may not be able to recover the secret language of numbers in its entirety, we shall explain it sufficiently to aid the student in his progress. We shall first endeavor to find out whether or not the formula of the ancients—All is in all—is correct. We will take the first phenomena at hand, the light of day for example, and see if we can find a law sufficiently general to exactly apply to phenomena of an entirely different order.

The day imposes the night, thus constituting the period of activity and repose which we find throughout nature. The opposition of light and darkness is the most marked phenomena in this consideration.

Observing it more closely, do we find this opposition absolute? We find the contrary. Between the period of absolute light and darkness we find on examination that which is neither light nor darkness, but partakes of the nature of both. This is called twilight.

When the light diminishes, the darkness increases as the latter depends upon a greater or less quantity of light. Darkness is but a modification of light. In order to discover the law hidden under these facts, we will generalize instead of using special terms. We may say two things entirely opposite in appearance have always an intermediate point common to both.

In the realm of the sexes we find the male opposed to the female. In physics, we find heat opposed to cold, positive to negative, etc. Law

—Between two opposites there is always an intermediary which partakes of the nature of both. First Fact—Male and female result, a child.

Second Fact—Solid state, gaseous state; intermediary result, liquid. Third Fact—Father and Son; intermediary, Holy Ghost. Second Law —The opposites are different only in the degree of perception.

HOW THE MYSTIC DIFFERS FROM THE MATERIALIST

YOU PROBABLY think of Consciousness as a living body with its normal senses working, taking moment by moment note of worldly activities going on around it. When a state is forced upon it that it no longer is taking note of activities going on around it, the acceptance of "unconsciousness" is general . . . even the state known as Death. But always it has to be some sort of organism, human or otherwise, that is conscious or unconscious. People become so accustomed to seeing or contacting the organic suit of clothes that the soul is wearing in any given life, that they forget the inner force that really is making the outer covering perform. To view this inner force, this Soul-Animation, as something with an identity unto itself, is asking the layman to deal in intangibles—that is, things of no substance. And in this world, generally speaking, things without substance are denied the fact of existence. Right there lies the big difference in thinking between the Materialist and the Mystic.

THE Materialist demands that the substantial organism shall be tangible to his five senses. The Mystic smiles tolerantly at the "hard and practical common senses" of the Materialist and asks, "What goes on then, when organic destruction results in Death and yet something provenly conscious continues to manifest?" Right there the Materialist abandons the "hard and practical common sense" for which he loves to be distinguished, goes into a vapor of generalities, concedes there is something called a Soul—which must be classified in the realm of Religion—and changes the subject to the increase of the interest rate on first mortgages. He is out of his depth, granted he had any depth in the first place.

THE MYSTIC, ages ago, had to erect the A structure of his thinking upon an entirely different premise. Of the two, the Mystic was truly the more practical, since he took into consideration all the phenomena of manifestation—and accounted for it—whereas the Materialist took into consideration only what he saw with his eyes or touched with his fingertips. The Mystic viewed the entire agenda of soul-demonstration, both in and out of the body, and drew the conclusion, "The Soul must exist since it performs under many conditions. It is probably possible, however, that its existence has to be proven through other means than the behavior of conscious organism. Being imperceptible to the senses by no means indicates its nonreality; perhaps it only means that Man lacks the equipment to see or contact it. The true fault isn't with the Soul but with the limitation of Man's equipment to behold the Soul."

So the Mystic went to work to study the performance of Soul as something independent of the instrument it might be using on any given plane, to arrive at some sort of understanding of Soul's composition. What he found, in the main, and over generations of time, was the challenging probability that Thought wasn't a mere observing and cogitating process of organic brain or mind, but that Thought could exist of, and by, itself. Thought could exist and perform independent of material organism, in other words. This was absolutely an original and independent Idea, altering the whole business of earthly logicizing.

THOUGHT wasn't a product of Substance a—say the substance of physical brain and nerves performing somehow within themselves to supply ideas to the organism that thereby was conscious. Substance, taken in any aspect one might come upon it or regard it, was a product of Thought. This gave the Materialist the facetious comment: "So you start with Nothing and get Something, is that it? and you call that sense?" To which the Mystic had to reply, "No, I don't start with Nothing and get Something.

I say that what you call Nothing is really in existence all the time but you declare it to be Nothing because you lack the equipment to perceive it. You merely say it is Nothing because it doesn't conform to the tests you place on Substance. It couldn't be Nothing and produce Something, because the fact that Something manifests proves its causes to have been equally in existence. This Something over which you make so much, merely responds to your organic sense equipment, thereby supplying the identity which you concede.

But my Nothing also has properties proving its existence. One of them is its ability to produce values that impact on your senses—the phenomenon which you call Something or Substance. Unless you concur in this, you are just as inconsistent as you claim I am, because your Something—in your logic—has come out of Nothing. For instance, all the materials making up the earthly universe—did they all derive from Nothing?

If you say they did, and were self-creating, then give me explanation for the mystery of Quantity. Why have there been limitations on amounts of something in existence? Why is our very planet the size it is? . . . why isn't it ten thousand times bigger, if it has been self-created? What has dictated that uranium, for instance, shall be a 'scarce' element? The Materialist cannot answer you, granted he follows you. His brain is already growing tired, he finds, trying to consider abstractions. But they are not abstractions. They are the soundest and hardest values existing in Nature, because they have produced an earth world in which one moves and needs sustenance. However, when trying to grasp what Life is—in order that average men and women may come to grasp what they themselves are—you have to pass from consideration of Substances in performance to consideration of Performance as an oddity unto itself. By investigating Performance you grope toward the core of the mystery of what the thing may be that is performing.

CONSCIOUSNESS, the capable Mystic says, is that paradox in Nature whose major attribute is being aware of itself and its functions. Being aware of itself requires that it must have or acquire a fair amount of individuality. This individuality in Consciousness we give the handy label of Soul. So long as we confine ourselves and attention to the finite unit possessed of no other attribute than self-awareness, that is one thing.

But the moment this Self-Aware Unit of Consciousness—or Soul—starts to do something extraneous to itself, meaning outside awareness of self and naught else, then we say it becomes Spirit. Spirit is Soul-in-Action, in other words. And Soul-in-Action takes the procedure of Thought to draw patterns or blueprints around which atoms assemble to give the material some things which the Materialist so dearly advocates. And the brain of Soul-in-Action, so to speak, performing the wonder of Thought Pattern-Making, is Mind. It may sound complicated to have these items so defined, but actually it is not.

Merely remember—in the universe Consciousness individualizes into particles that give us souls. Each is distinguished by its ability to be aware of its own existence—to itself. The moment it thinks outside of this self-awareness and in terms of conveying its self-awareness to other souls, it translates into Spirit, or soul performing externally. And it conveys this existence of itself and self-awareness to other units by activities known as Thinking and the designs it works in materials through thinking. And the instrument it employs for all such performing's is Mind.

Get this simple line of definitions and you begin to acquire the very basic knowledge of the Mystics of all the ages, who have worked such marvels of control of Mind over Matter. They have worked such marvels because first of all they got their reasoning and identifying sorted out as to the exact meaning and activities implied in each of these terms. Furthermore, we find ourselves on sound terrain in so accepting each as described, because they do account for all the supernatural as well as the natural phenomena we encounter on the various octaves of reality, including the earthly. And to it we should add, the new science of nuclear fission backs these terms up as well, and supplies explanations for the mystery of Quantity in materials. Especially pious mystics, by the way, call this great cosmic reservoir of Consciousness—that can individualize itself into particles known as Souls —the Mind of God, or Divine Mind.

It is a pretty term, but it can also alienate the mental scientist and logician who is searching for what happens in soul-creation, and therefore what men and women are when souls imbed in organism.

THERE IS, in the universe, a principle that is capable of self-awareness and that over gradual periods of time in each instance acquires Individuality. Confined to self-awareness only, each of such particles is just a Soul—that could go on contemplating itself so for millions of years if it chose. But really that wouldn't mean very much unless it manifested to other self-contemplating souls, and the instant it does so it is recognized as, and named spirit. In other words, it is known as a spirit. Visiting earthly organism again and again, experience comes to it that emphasizes such individuality until personality begins to be acquired, Finally it exercises such soul-spirit through powers of Thought and creates what are known as Thought-Forms, which are truly thought-patterns for atoms to adhere around.

Thereby docs Thought actually create Matter and material objects or substances . . . and the Materialist is left far behind in it all, scarcely grasping "what it is all about". . . It isn't a mere esoteric or mystical theory, formulated to alibi or rationalize what Thought can provenly do in effecting Materials. But whether it is or not, when the Materialist begins to follow what the Mystic has explored and found to be true, he has to abandon all his previous notions and start a new line of thinking, because he discovers that the Mystic's ideas concretely work The point we are interested in making at the moment, however, is What Life Is to Start With.

Life to start with, is Divine Mind "thinking" in terms of distinct and individual particles of Consciousness, with the patterns in which it thinks exercising or expressing according to the species or specimen of the created thing. As these particles become more and more aware of themselves and then more and more positive about external functions, they become creators of inanimate substance in their own rights.

Such is the premise from which all miracle-workers operate. You might read ten thousand books on Mysticism, but they wouldn't tell you one syllable more than is contained in the foregoing exposition. Get the foregoing understanding in your head and you have started your intellect on its way to understanding of all the phenomena in the Natural Universe. It is not so particularly complicated. What it is, is different.

THIS WORLD EXISTS
You Realize You Are

LIFE IN all the world systems, no matter where or in what form we find it, has but a single intent and purpose, a single meaning and method, a single power and wholeness. That is self-awareness or the knowing of itself as being in existence along with die knowing of its own traits and conduct. So we seem to be told from every level of conscious Thought, no matter how far souls of vast age have probed into it.

This is doubly true of life in its mortal—or human—form where the idea is to make the soul know that it is, what it is, and what it can become.

MEN SHOULD get this idea so firmly fixed in their minds that they use it as the cornerstone in all their reasoning. Perfect self-awareness is the nub of the universe as men know it. Inorganic matter and organic matter, mussel life or granite rock, to the highest and finest flower of Christ or super-angel, the purpose of life in each instance is first to know that it is, then grasp the full chances and powers in existence at a state of growth, or a goal, that is called Cosmic Consciousness—or a full knowledge of all the consciousness there is, also known as The Absolute.

WHEN we talk about Cosmic Consciousness and The Absolute, we find ourselves dealing with terms that carry few picture-images to our minds and sooner or later we begin to lose interest in our subject. When a discourse stops dealing with mental pictures, or images, that can be pulled up in the mind's eye, we say that it is dull. And we are right. If God gave us minds that work in pictures and images, why despise them and think that we are somehow clever in dropping them and trying to think without them?

The growing schoolboy loves to argue in this fashion and fancy that he is profound. Scholars with bulging foreheads discard the picture method and try to go on with ten-pound words, leaving it to the technical meaning of those words and not the mental images they call up, to get the sense of their logic across. Somehow they think that this proves their grey matter. But the truly profound scholar keeps to simple words and pictures, as Jesus did.

Even today Jesus keeps His speech to words of one and two syllables, and so His following is vast because He is easily understood. But where is the scholar, youthful or mature, who can answer the question, where did Life come front in the first place? and hold his treatise down to plain and simple terms?

THE WILL at once define Life as "gradations of Evolution" and going back over them, one before the other, he will come to a First Cause which he will call "cosmological propagation." What will he be doing but playing on words and admitting his own ignorance of the true root of the universe? The scholar who is honest will say, "Life comes out of the God Principle and that is unknowable." That is to say, he thinks it is unknowable because he gets the wrong idea of what the God Principle may be in its process of display.

SUPPOSE that we put it in this manner—God, meaning of course Holy Spirit, was, is, and ever will be, a condition within the universe, or throughout the universe, that has nothing to do with Time and Space, but is a form of all-embracing Consciousness of which ideas are a display of its self-awareness. That is to say, Holy Spirit made itself aware of itself by becoming what we might call an "introvert" after a fashion, looking into itself, wondering what was there, and producing a universe in order to find out.

This, of course, is hard for mankind to grasp, for men must always have a sense of their own limitations about them to make them aware that they are men at all. In other words, men must always have a Cause before an Effect.

But Holy Spirit, being both Cause and Effect in this instance, urged itself into knowing itself and thus wrought the universe as we know it by "speaking a word". . .

Not an actual word, we mean, spoken by an actual tongue, but a desire to pry within its own Idea-System that should, by the years of events, make one part of itself seen and known to every other part.

OR PUT it in this way—The things that Holy Spirit did as ideas, it still docs or is doing as ideas. One o these ideas is our world of reality out of which grows a knowledge of everything that there is to know, or Cosmic Consciousness. Or put it in a third way: God wrought Himself out of Himself in order to make one sort of idea understandable to itself as separate and distinct from every other sort of idea, each likewise knowing itself.

Do we seem to be saying the same thing over and over? Well, we have to recall that that is exactly what Life itself is doing to us, moment by moment and eon by eon, until we not only accept it but all at once start to be it.

WITH that out in 'inky-black Space,' without form or limit, there was an *Idea Being* that said to itself—"Here am I, entrapped as a person of a sort, without the chance to go anywhere, do anything, or be anything other than I am. I want to express Myself to Myself. Since there is nothing outside of Myself, I must get all this display within myself. I will therefore explore Myself and find out how many kinds and divisions of ideas go to make Me up."

Now the falseness of thinking of Holy Spirit as a being like a man or an animal, lies in the difference between what the scholar calls "objectivity and subjectivity," or as we will put it, in the difference between all that is outside and all that is inside.

The Holy Spirit, as we are striving to grasp it in all respect and devoutness, is pure and complete Subjectivity. That is, all that exists for it, lies within itself. You can grasp a mind picture of what this means when you try to imagine a universe without a single idea in it. It would be, in a manner of speaking, Total Nothingness. Now as all ideas are traits of the Holy Spirit, we should not have trouble in grasping how all that is, is within the Holy Spirit.

So we might put it, God is the universe that is within itself.

And because we can't conceive of any sort of universe lying outside the pale of ideas, so in no sense or part is He a being that has anything whatever to do with anything outside or beyond Himself. If we want to toy with the notion that there is anything Unknowable about Holy Spirit, it is this strange item: that such an Idea-Being could exist and get a result like the universe—of which all of us, on all planes of existence, are conscious parts.

IN OUR various worlds of Substance in Matter, that came into being because Thought sent forth Energy and got form and substance, it would indeed be absurd. It would be absurd because everything that exists in our mortal universe is the result of the process. As mortal souls, everything in our universe is outside ourselves—our true soul-selves, even our physical bodies.

Perhaps you can begin to grasp from this that we are the exact opposite in display from Holy Spirit, that reverses the process or condition and has everything inside it. If you will stop and think about it, you will see that the only way we compare with Holy Spirit—proving that we too are little bits of Holy Spirit—is in the fact that if we have anything truly within ourselves it is ideas, or a little reservoir of ideas that as yet haven't taken display in any form of Matter.

WE MEET with a sort of mental distress in trying to think of existence that is wholly within ourselves, and thus confined within limits. For at once we start asking: "Well, and good, but something must lie outside of those bounds, and what is it?" Now those who have lived and "died," and lived and "died," into finer and finer degrees of Thought and Matter, over thousands of life-cycles, and gotten deeper and deeper into the very core of spirit-creation, have grasped a knowledge of something that mortal men haven't—*That the universe is not limitless in bounding it by length, breadth, and depth.*

Does an Idea, taken of and by itself, have length, breadth, or depth? Of course not. It is a thing that belongs to the mind of the spirit, not something of touchable materials.

So we have God, or Holy Spirit, existing as a lengthless, breadthless, and depthless Being, able to know itself as a great basic urge, or a reservoir of fruitful Idea-Beings, which when broken up or displayed in forms of substance result in objects having length, breadth, and depth.

Consider it in this way again—The universe has no bounds, being a mass of unborn ideas, or ideas that haven't yet had a chance to display in Matter, all bound up in the Mammoth Idea of possible creation of objects. This Mammoth Idea is not a boundable thing. All is contained within it, no matter how far its contents extend. Even Space as we know it would be a part of the contents of the Idea. In that sense it is limitless. It is not limitless, however, when it comes to a display of its contents. For there are only so many ideas making it up. You must not confuse measurement with formless Thought. That is just what you do when you try to grasp the universe as a place.

THERE ARE places within the universe, it is true, and they may be ten trillion Lightyear's from one another. Still, the pattern of the Idea behind them is limited and in that sense we get limitation. Then again, this thing seems to happen—A point is reached where the universe "runs out of ideas," so to speak, and when it does that, it has to come back to its first Self-Evidence which was its wholeness.

Therefore, in a manner of speaking, it "meets itself" and beyond that there is no thinking.

DO NOT become confused here. You think of ideas as fancies taking some sort of form. Those on far, far levels of spirit think of ideas as terms in which forms can display. You will see the difference if you stop to think about it a moment. Ideas come to you in your mortal universe from the angles of higher levels of conscious Thought and you receive them in the mortal world as channels and tools for grasping the various forms of conduct in Matter.

But behind them all there is still a basic Principle of Limitation. An idea carried far enough through all the processes of thinking and displaying, finally arrives at itself again. Some of your scientists on the earth-side therefore put it, from this truth, that after going outward for a certain distance, the universe fold s back in upon itself. And insofar as they express what happens to the limit of ideas, they are quite correct.

HOLY SPIRIT does not want to know itself in order to be clever, or to create a display of itself to relieve any boredom in its self-awareness. It seeks some form of display by

Thought performing in and through and by *Energy* and getting *Matter*, that its separate parts may have a clearer knowledge of what the *Whole* is made up of—and what is in the Whole. Thus it is a self-educating Holy Spirit, if you want to view it from the angle of any one of its separate parts.

Having reached this pass in our thinking for the moment, suppose we go back and take up the Life Principle as a germ within Holy Spirit to be brought into a greater sense of self-awareness and thus the awareness of the universe of which it is a needful part. Perhaps in the workings of the Life Principle toward this end, we shall catch a glimpse of what goes on in the Body Brain-Mind of Holy Spirit as a great reservoir of ideas performing within itself. . .

NOW THE Life Principle seems to be this: Realizing what part of the Divine Idea it either is, or can be! Life in this sense is a sort of "resentment" of all other parts making up the whole—a kind of protest, so to speak, that there are other parts, and by its protest grasping that it exists. Universal consciousness has a queer way of folding in upon itself, we have seen, after the pattern we have just had spread before us. Now it is a fact that you can't have conscious Thought in the abstract—that is, without Ego, or some sort of Self considered as a seat of consciousness. But you can have this queer process—

You can have an idea so powerful in its possibilities for displaying itself that it works a lodestone effect on that which is about it. When you have done this, you have gotten Motion of a sort. And out of this Motion, or energy displaying, comes every known substance and material. But here is the startling thing that we learn on these higher levels of conscious thought: You don't get substance and materials at once out of energy, or from Energy. That is, directly. You get the last thing in the world that mortal scholars suspect of being a step in the process. You get Light!

Remember the four steps: first, conscious Thought that is a display on the part of that great reservoir of ideas, the Holy Spirit; second, ideas within it so powerful in possibilities for displaying themselves in form that they evolve Energy; third, Energy resulting in the miracle known as Light; fourth, Light assembling particles of what for the present we must call

Ether, and getting substance or matter materials.

THIS PUZZLES you, no doubt. Why Light? We shall see further on in another paper. Light must have a separate paper unto itself, and when we say Light we mean vastly more, of course, than the common forms of vibratory incandescence visible to mortal eve. But grasp this now if you can—

"The idea back of the universe is not a fancy that comes from a Brain-Mind outside the mortal world and thrust into it. It is an effect produced within itself, containing no item that works against its display as a perfect idea, and having within itself the power to propel itself into forms of display that can be noted by its own senses". . .

But, you ask, how can a mere "mental notion" of itself, bring about hard, actual, substantial matter? How can the mere idea of a granite monument, for example, existing first as the Thought-Notion of a monument, finally appear as a hundred tons of stone that mangles you beyond repair when you crash into it in a fast-moving automobile? Your question is a fair one. But we answer you, the explanation is twofold and both parts of it lie within your question itself. We will try to show you what we mean—

FIRST, IN thinking that ideas are mere "mental notions," unborn as to form and substance in Matter, you are not grasping the true nature of the conscious Thought that makes ideas what they seem to be to you. Second, in thinking of "hard, actual, substantial matter" you are taking it to be something which we declare to you it is not.

In the first place, you grasp a knowledge of what an idea is, or what makes an idea, from somewhere, and by a similar trait in your own consciousness that exists in Universal Thought, you fashion a picture or image and call the result a mere "mental notion."

Can you not grasp the fact that ideas may have a form of reality harder than the hardest granite in the hardest monument to begin with, and that what you behold in your mind as a mere "mental notion" may be nothing but the mirrored reflection of a true reality already in existence?

In other words, what you call the mental notion has come about because your consciousness has played the role of looking-glass, only instead of the image striking the surface as it comes from the actual thing and being reflected so that it is seen in front of the looking glass, it goes through, so to speak, and is wholly absorbed and kept by the looking-glass and known as an existing image only by the looking-glass.

YOU SAY to us, frowning and pursing your lips, "All right, as a neat way to squirm out in logic. But after all, where is the real thing that is thus reflected? Whereabouts does it exist?" We say to you, "It doesn't exist anywhere in the form that will ultimately kill you if your car crashes into it as into the monument. That will be the property it takes when it displays in the mortal form that you can know with your mortal senses. None the less, the idea as an idea, in its own element, may be quite as real as when it displays in your clement, which is so-called adamant substance."

And yet, while we are on the subject, Matter is not actually a substance that can be defined outside of an Idea.

What would you say, for instance, if you were soberly told that there are levels of consciousness above the mortal where an Idea can run you down and wangle you exactly like the motorcar that we mentioned as carrying you straight toward the towering obelisk?

"RUN DOWN by an idea?" you cry. "Nonsense!" But it's not nonsense if your consciousness too worked only in a form that was of the stuff that "dreams are made of". . .

After all, what is Matter that pushes you, and pinches you, and falls on your toes, and fractures your skulls? It is merely a property of the universe that has the power to affect you consciously thus, because you too are operating in a similar property or on a similar plane of vibratory substance.

WE HAVE heard people with wits enough in other mental problems, so that they ought to be able to admit this instantly, scoff and scorn at this offering of the facts and say—"That's all very well, but such a stating of the case implies that all of us can exist as Ideas in a universe of Pure Ideas."

They say it as though there were something childish, silly, absurd or disreputable about such a universe.

You go to bed at night and fall asleep. Along toward dawn you commence to dream. While you are in the dream, the world in which you move is just as real to you for all practical purposes of sensing and knowing as the world of Matter to which you will shortly awaken. The people you meet are quite as nice, quite as sane, and perhaps a whole lot nicer and saner than those you will confront on tumbling out of bed. You may argue that you create that world and people in it. Well, what if you do? You suffer and exult just as much, as a result of these creations, as you do in meeting with the world of actual Matter made for you first by Divine Consciousness.

You learn to be a successful and distinct idea yourself by taking your form and cues out of Divine Mind. And the only way that Divine Mind can demonstrate, or show what those forms, cues, and other possibilities are, is to project a universe of substance in Matter: the material world as we know it.

SCIENCE OF OCCULT HEALING

An ancient legend with much beauty of imagery tells us of a wonderful, luminous pearl that was taken from the world and dropped into the unfathomable depths of an enveloping ocean. Its brilliance was thus lost for ages. At last a winged host of faithful birds from many regions, instead of waiting for time to dry up the ocean, carried away the water in their bills drop by drop with ever increasing patience and persistence. Thus was the long lost gem recovered amid universal rejoicing.

The imagery of this legend echoes the story of your divine birth and progress, and mine, too, friend and reader. In an ocean of enveloping Omnipresence the priceless gem of Omniscience is hidden within you and me and we have been endowed with a sufficiency of latent Omnipotence to enable us to carry away before us, drop by drop the separating sea of ignorance that lies between us and the priceless jewel of spiritual Wisdom. This is our divine heritage and it will eventually and naturally be ours when the demands of involution, being sufficiently satisfied, the consummatory and spiritual processes of evolution will be possible to us.

But you and I are not waiting for time's sequence of events to bring us the necessary alchemical experiences to bestow upon us the gift of wisdom. We are no longer evolving unconsciously, but consciously. We are striving to delve deeper than those beatific experiences of mysticism which so long have satisfied the stage of progress when emotion, while dominating the intelligence, seeks to lift us from the lower to the higher, and does it, too, in flaming ecstasies. But at this later stage we wish to add the scientific experiences of occultism, that they may raise us higher still in bliss and register in the realms of reason, with intuitions seal upon them, the truths which we have learned. Thus shall we become the perfect Wisdom which is eternal, not only possess knowledge which is ephemeral.

The intensity and one-pointedness of our will to know, the courage of our convictions and the unselfishness of our purpose, are the things upon which depend the time it will require for us to attain our heritage of perfect Wisdom. It is not to be gained in a little while, a few years, a lifetime or even in a few lives. It requires an eternity of time and I feel sure that even when we shall have become worthy to stand face to face, after the long ages of the 'glass darkly,' we shall let fall our glance feeling our ignorance and imperfections. Realizing this we should probably grow discouraged because of our limitations and imperfect faculties, were there not so much joy in striving and in the ideal we cherish of serving others. The facts which we are to consider together, I have searched for and studied for many, many years; and now the science of occultism is to me such a natural, practical and helpful thing, that my heart and mind overflow into The Channel. I hope that other serious students may be glad to make use of these facts, which have made my life stream on with such surety and understanding of the laws of being.

In our study together I hope we may come close in sympathetic and personal relationship. I shall speak frankly and hope you will receive it in the spirit in which it is offered. The student who is earnest and conscientious and whose life is consecrated to the service of humanity, need not fear misunderstanding and ridicule in these days, when there is such a keen, universal desire to come closer to nature's laws and work with them, while bringing the intelligence and reason to bear upon the problems which confront us.

In the Middle Ages, the occultist took for his motto: "To will, to dare, to do and to keep silent," the last dictum being necessary to protect his life from ridicule and to save his head from the scaffold. But now his motto reads otherwise. For the occultist of today the scaffold is no longer erected and he has lost the fear of ridicule; above all he is ordered to assist in the dissemination of truth for the helping of humanity. Therefore he forgets himself and wills, dares, does—and speaks, fearing naught.

We shall study first the interesting subject of occult healing. The time has come when we must try to reach to the outermost circle of vague healing generalities and bring them into a center of scientific and particular application. We must study the laws and forces which lie on the inner planes of nature and which we use consciously or unconsciously in our healing endeavors. It seems to me that persons are very unwise in using healing power without understanding what they are doing and the nature of the forces they are using. It is my hope to describe these forces to you and to suggest a more rational and practical method of their application. I do not think we can know each other too well since we are thus to work together, and our motive must be pure—the hope of more effectually alleviating the world's pain. So I trust you will let me tell you how long I have been interested in the subject and what I have learned while studying it.

Let us go back to my childhood, when I was already suffering 'growing pains'—perhaps you were too. If we have made early history of an approximately similar kind, we shall be sympathetic students, and please let me find you also possessed of a ready sense of humor, for I believe that to be a necessary qualification for those pursuing our special line of study. It is such a good crutch upon which our commonsense can lean and balance itself, as we go hobbling along our difficult road. It is not just for people to think it necessary that the occultist be a gloomy, weird, peculiar person, aloof from the practical paths or joys of life.

The true occultist is other. He is not the strange, fantastic person whose reputation needs to be defended by long disheveled hair, if he be a man; or, if a woman, short cropped and unkempt locks and garments of an antiquated or strange pattern. These things are more prevalent in the false or pseudo-occultist who must attract attention by unusual outer things, because lacking the inner graces of intelligence and order, of which the outer is ever the reflection. A witty friend calls him the mockultist; his prose tragedy unsmiling countenance, punctuated with large round mysterious eyes and far-away expression, fails to be a mask to those who understand such types and who know that there is nothing to warrant such an appearance on the part of anyone. Another great obstacle to the study of occultism is an awesome fear of what is mistakenly called supernatural. There is nothing supernatural in the whole scheme of things.

Super-physical yes, but even so, very tangible and real, with practical laws governing it, which we can understand and obey. The true occultist is beyond the stage of evolution where one works out his 'salvation with fear and trembling', or thinks that 'fear is the beginning of wisdom'. The savage does feel a superstitious terror of what appears to him as the super-natural since he lacks intelligence; with him terror exists as a punitive agent and moral necessity to awaken his sense of good and evil.

But knowledge removes from our life structure, the scaffolding of fear which has been unconsciously erected about it during these earlier stages of evolution. And at present we shall build with confidence, working out our 'salvation' in minds and hearts where will and love have supplanted awesome fear and trembling. Let us again turn to my childhood days of which I spoke a few minutes ago. Did your early life, as mine, have various cycles which opened and for a time enveloped an all-absorbing subject, and then closed up tight again, mercilessly ruled by time and circumstance?

One of these disclosed the subject of healing to my yearning childish heart and groping mind, when I was barely eight. There is a vivid memory of a day when I returned from Sunday school after hearing for the first time of Christ's miracles of healing. These were the details of His life that spoke the most appealingly to my imagination as I thought of the marvelous results of His ministering love and felt the love, reverence and gratitude of those who were healed. I fled to a corner of the garden in my father's home and threw myself down on the grass under an apple tree, almost beside myself with joy. My childish mind painted endless pictures of those wondrous miracles—the crowds that followed Christ, the suffering throngs of people who desired to be healed and the demonstrations of gratitude and reverence by those who had been made whole. Finally, by the sheer bursting of my heart, I was forced to talk to someone about it all. I rushed into the lap of my dear father—my confidant and friend—and seizing him by the lapels of his coat and bumping my forehead against his breast, I cried: "Tell me how Christ healed! Tell me quick for I must know so that I can cure Julia's measles." Julia was my five year old idol sister. My father's astonishment had time to subside during my repeated demand.

Then I breathlessly waited for the explanation, feeling sure that it would come from one so wise as he; "My child, only One as holy as the Christ can heal the sick as he did." What a disappointing blow to my enthusiasm! The flood-gates of my childish emotion were let loose and the tears fell in torrents for a long time. The agony of my discouragement lasted far into the next day; but little by little my hope returned and stealthily, with deep determination, I laid a plot, resolving to cure Julia in spite of everything. I felt somehow, somewhere that I could accomplish it, and that father must have been mistaken when he said that only Christ could heal. The greater part of the following day was spent in suppressed excitement with many pilgrimages to the apple tree, while renewing courage to carry out my plan.

I told no one of it fearing ridicule if it were known. From my little Bible I read over and over again the healing miracles and about Christ raising Lazarus from the dead. I said aloud many times the prayer, "Father I thank Thee that Thou hast heard me," but my mind was too ignorant to understand the secret of the occult power in those words. Then I crept softly through the garden to a side door, and into Julia's room where she lay sleeping. I slipped under her little crib and began shrieking: "Get up Julia! Get up Julia! Carry your crib to father and tell him you are well. Take up your crib and walk!" Over and over I screamed the words. A whole harvest of mustard seeds of faith was in that cry. I paused in breathless suspense waiting for her to obey me. Alas! the miniature mountains of measles did not remove themselves one bit but were deaf to my command. Julia did not get up, but with a loud scream covered up her little head in fright. I saw her thus instead of being healed, as my dear father hauled me out by my heels and carried me away to his room.

Truly the most discouraging lessons are often those learned through our failures, but they also frequently test the strength of our purpose. In great contrition I confessed to him my doubts of his assurance that only Christ could heal and that I had determined to try it myself. I told him it did not seem right for God to allow so much illness, suffering and death in the world and yet give only one person the power to heal them; I did not believe Him so unjust and therefore I determined to go about curing people myself.

Never shall I forget the expression of yearning sadness on that loved face as he tenderly made me understand that such a thing was impossible for me, that God had not revealed the mysteries of healing to us and that we must not question His wisdom for keeping us in ignorance. Oh! the resentment my sad, devoted childish heart cherished towards the One who would keep anything secret from my father. For days I could not be induced to say my bedside prayer. My youthful reasoning heaped up such a pile of evidence against the justice of an all-loving creator that my father found considerable difficulty in answering satisfactorily the heretical attacks of my young mind and heart. Finally he pleaded an alibi. Holding me close to his heart he suggested that by prayer we would endeavor to make God understand that we desired Him to take us more into His confidence, and in order sufficiently to give vent to my pent-up feelings he allowed me to find fault with God for His apparent selfishness in keeping all these things to Himself, when the world needed them so much.

Then, in the days that followed, he gradually led me back to a more becoming attitude of reverential supplication. So we prayed on through long years, with hopes high and minds confident. Friend, do not think me egotistical when I say that the prayer was answered. Little by little I have been able through study and persistent endeavor to erase from my mind and heart that pile of evidence against divine justice which was stored up in my childhood's irreverent ignorance. Not only that but in its place there has been heaped up a far greater mass of facts to the contrary. This has convinced me that the Divine laws of life are just, especially when considered from the viewpoint and experience of the occultist who is constantly using them and testing their justice and efficiency. Occult healing is one of the branches of work wherein it is possible to test these laws fully. My researches have produced results which are indisputable and this has been true of many earnest students besides myself.

Moreover, knowledge of these laws places the power to heal on a much more accurate basis of scientific application than would otherwise be possible. Twenty-five years of studying it and other occult subjects have resulted in steadily increasing my enthusiasm and interest. Also it is such a joy to have proven that superstition, fatalism, agnosticism and atheism have no true bases of facts, but exist only as the offspring of ignorance. In subsequent chapters I shall outline a rational method of healing based upon the practical and scientific application of occult law. But first let me review the results of personal experiences gained while studying Christian Science, New Thought, Suggestion, Psychology, Mental Science, Psychoanalysis and Psycho-diagnosis, and many other philosophies. This review is necessary for the purposes of study, comparison and analysis. It will not be made in a spirit of unkind criticism, as that is against my principles, but in the effort to understand truth in whatever form it may be found.

DIVINE WILL

THERE is only one will in the universe just as there is only one mind. The one mind is the mind of God, the one will is the will of God. The mind of individual man is an individual or differentiated expression of the Infinite mind, and the largeness of this human mind depends upon how much of the one mind man may decide to appropriate. Man has the freedom to incorporate in his own individual consciousness as much of the Infinite mind as he may desire; and as the mind of the Infinite is limitless, the mind of man may continue to become larger and larger without any end.

The will of the individual mind is a partial expression of the will of God, just as the force of growth that is in each branch is a part of the same force that is in the vine, and the power of the individual will depends upon how perfectly the individual mind works in harmony with the Infinite mind. There is no limit to the power of the will of God, the divine will; therefore, when the human will is as large a part of the divine will as the individual mind can appropriate and apply, the human will necessarily becomes immensely strong; and since the individual mind can appropriate a larger and a larger measure of the divine will, there is no limit to the power of will that can be developed in the mind of man.

To develop the true will, the first essential is to realize that there is but one will, and that we will with the one will just as we live the one life and think with the one mind, though in our thinking, living and willing, we do not, as a rule, do justice to that part of the whole which it is our privilege to use. We think, live and will too much as isolated entities instead of as divine beings eternally united with the Supreme. The second essential is to realize that the divine will works only for better things and greater things. The path of the divine will is upward and onward forever, and its power is employed exclusively in building more lofty mansions for the soul.

Therefore the will of God does not produce sickness, adversity or death; on the contrary, the will of God eternally wills to produce wholeness, harmony and life. The ills of personal life are not produced by divine will;

they are produced by man's inability to properly use that part of divine will that is being expressed in his mind, and this inability comes because man does not always apply his will in harmony with divine will. When man uses his will as his own isolated power, he separates his mind more and more from the source of his power; in consequence, the power of his will becomes weaker, and he necessarily fails to accomplish what he has in view. He also falls apart from the one ascending current of life; he gets out of harmony with the true order of things, and sickness, trouble, adversity and want invariably follow.

The true use of the will is to apply the will in the full recognition of the oneness of the human will with the divine will. My will is as much of the divine will as I am using now, and it is my privilege to use as much of the divine will as I may desire. To constantly think of my will and the divine will as the same will, is to place my mind in such perfect harmony with the limitless power of divine will that I can appropriate this power in larger and larger measure, and the more I appropriate, the stronger becomes the power of will in me. When the individual mind is in such perfect harmony with the Supreme mind that the divine will can be given free and full expression, the will of the individual mind becomes invincible; the secret therefore of developing a powerful will is found here, and here alone.

The true will is never domineering nor antagonistic; neither does it ever apply the force of resistance. If you are antagonistic or have a tendency to resist everything that is not to your liking, it is proof conclusive that you are not in harmony with divine will. You are misdirecting your power, and are forming obstacles and pitfalls for yourself. The divine will does not attempt to overcome evils and obstacles with antagonistic or domineering forces; the divine will does not fight wrong, it transforms wrong. It works in silence and serenity, but goes so deeply into the elements of things that it undermines the very first causes of all adverse or detrimental conditions. It does not resist the surface, but goes calmly beneath the surface and transforms those undercurrents from which surface conditions proceed. The divine will, by going into the deeper life of all things, transforms all things into harmony with itself; and it can transform all things because its power is supreme.

Therefore when we are in the midst of adversity, we should not rail against fate nor antagonize those conditions that seem to work against us. We have within us the power of divine will, and this will can change everything for good. But it not only can, it will. It is not the will of God to keep any person in adversity. It is the will of God to set every person free, and every person will be set free when he places his life completely in the hands of divine will. When the individual mind can say, from the heart, Thy will be done, the individual life has been placed in the power of divine will and that life will at once begin to pass out of adversity, sickness, trouble and want, into the world of freedom.

However, we do not give up our individuality when we give our mind over to divine will; we do not become automatons in the hands of some superior power; on the contrary, we open our minds to that power that alone can produce individuality. The individuality we now possess has been formed by whatever measure of divine will that we have incorporated in our own conscious existence, and by opening our minds completely to divine will, we shall gain sufficient power to make our individuality infinitely stronger and superior to what it now is. Our purpose is not to be used by the Supreme, but to use the power of the Supreme. To live the life of God, think the thought of God, and will with the will of God—that is the secret path to the highly developed individuality; and it is such an individuality that becomes a master mind, a Son of the Most High. When the individual mind declares, Thy will be done, consciousness must fully recognize the presence of Supreme power, and must realize, with depth of thought and feeling, that Supreme power invariably leads to higher ground—the world of freedom and superior existence.

When the mind gives up to divine will in an indifferent, submissive, self-surrendering attitude, it is not giving up to divine will; it is simply giving up to the surrounding forces of fate. Such a mind will permit the forces of adversity to have their way, thinking that it is the will of God that much suffering must still be endured, and will consequently drift with circumstances, accepting whatever comes as a necessary chastisement. This method, however, weakens the mind, and places the individual more out of harmony with God than ever before. We always place ourselves out of harmony with God when we accept evil as coming from Him, and we weaken our own ability to use divine will when we permit adversity to exist thinking that it was sent from God.

To give the mind over to divine will is not to give up at all, in the ordinary sense of that term; we simply place ourselves in that position where we can use the power of the one true will instead of a mere imitation. We blend our own desires and aims with that power that we KNOW can see us through, and we work in the realization that whatever is detrimental in our plans will be eliminated as we press on towards the great goal in view. The mind that is aimless, waiting for the will of God to take him where he belongs, will drift with fate. He is not in the hands of divine will, he is in the hands of circumstances because he has not given divine will something to do. God does not tell us what to do; He has given us the wisdom to know our own desires and our own tendencies, and He has given us the power to fulfil those desires, but we must take individual action; this is why we have individuality and free individual choice.

However, when we do take individual action, God will work with us if we enter into harmony with Him, and when He is with us, failure is impossible. To use divine will, we must first have a lofty purpose in view; we must have something high and something definite that we wish to attain; we must have something upon which to apply the limitless power of divine will, and we must desire to reach that goal with the very deepest and strongest desires of heart and soul. Then we must will to press on, knowing that we are using divine will, the Supreme will of the Most High, because this is the only will in the universe. It is the will that eternally wills the higher, the greater and the better the will that is invincible, and always does what it wills to do.

FINIS

For those interested in Rosicrucian or similar Esoteric teachings.

Soul.org
theosophical.org
whiteaglelodge.org
PTTHfoundation.com

www.ingramcontent.com/pod-product-compliance
Ingram Content Group UK Ltd.
Pitfield, Milton Keynes, MK11 3LW, UK
UKHW020222250726
13967UKWH00001B/137

9 780359 122172